BUILDING RELATIONAL DATABASES MADE EASY

Database development
for ordinary people

M. CLINTON JONES

Building Relational Databases Made Easy: Database Development For Ordinary People
M. Clinton Jones

This edition published 2014 by Diogenes Academic Press

Diogenes Academic Press is an imprint of Bristol Folk Publications
www.bristol–folk.co.uk

ISBN 13: 978–1–909953–56–7

Jacket design copyright © Diogenes Academic Press 2014
Digital layout and realisation by Diogenes Academic Press
Jacket painting © Iorwerth Tosca 2014

USE OF MICROSOFT COPYRIGHTED CONTENTS

All screenshots of Microsoft Access 2013 used with permission from Microsoft. All screenshots comply with Microsoft's terms and conditions for use, which do not allow use of partial screenshots. Therefore, for many images the Window has been resized so as to show relevant detail, which is allowable under Microsoft's terms and conditions of use. Please note that layout of items shown in screenshots may therefore be different when viewed in full Windows.

CONTENTS

About the author

It was a rubber–keyed Spectrum that introduced M. Clinton Jones to IT. He bought said computer in the mid–1980s to document his then sprawling progressive jazz, folk and rock vinyl record collection. He discovered quickly what 48K meant; he only got as far as *Can* before the Spectrum started randomly transposing characters because it couldn't cope with the sheer volume of data. It went back in the box.

In 1994 he tried his hand with IT again and left behind the drudgery of the NHS (eleven years of mopping blood from operating theatre floors) to enrol on an introductory computing course. He progressed by slow turns to getting that degree he'd always promised himself – First Class with Honours, no less – which led to a teaching job at his old university, though, if truth be known he was already teaching there even before he got his degree. Many years later he now teaches database development (amongst other things) at the University of Bristol.

His first foray into print was in *The Rough Guide to Rock*, 3rd edition (Penguin/Rough Guides) in 1998, whilst back in academia he co–wrote several journal papers and a conference paper. He is vaguely annoyed that his academic contributions all appear as *et al* in most popular referencing styles. Other highlights include contributing to a Government White Paper on the IT Infrastructure Library (ITIL) and writing for various magazines and journals on subjects as diverse as music and railways.

In 2009 his first book, *Bristol Folk*, was published. *The Guardian* and the *English Folk Dance and Song Society* (and many others) said nice things about it. Subsequent books on various aspects of music (and railway sound recording) history all received excellent reviews and one, *The B&C Discography*, was recently nominated for an international excellence in musical history award. At time of going to press he has no idea if his book is amongst the winners. He'll know in September 2014.

He doesn't talk about his, so far, one–off detour into children's fiction, not that he used his real name for that one. Not that it is really for children either. There might be a second volume.

Meanwhile, the 20th anniversary of his introduction to databases seems a fitting time to present his own contribution to database development. And here it is.

FOREWORD

This book gives a good shaking to the myth that building relational databases is *difficult*. Nothing could be further from the truth – that is once you ignore all of the unnecessary information thrown at you by most software–specific *how–to–build–databases* books and all of the software features that you'll never need to touch.

Instead of selling you software features, this book shows you clearly and plainly what you need to do to build *any* database from a paper–based relational database design. It does this by using the BATS Technique©, which concentrates on the *building blocks* required for building databases without getting side–tracked along the way by neat stuff that you can do with so and so's software, but which doesn't actually get your job done.

What this book doesn't do in any depth is cover how to *use* your database once it's built – there are plenty of books, YouTube videos and other web–based resources that you can use to find out how to manage your data. This book is concerned with getting your database built and not much else.

Using your database, once you've built it, needs a very different set of skills to those used in either the design or development stages. That said, simple examples of creating queries and a report are included just to get you started. If you don't know what queries and reports are, don't worry, we'll cover this before we get started with the development work.

Building Relational Databases Made Easy is one of those books I wish I'd had twenty years ago. It must be said that I was a bit of a diva when it came to designing databases, even more so once I hit upon my patent TONTO Technique©, but building the things was another matter altogether. Luckily, I've got much better at the building side over the intervening twenty years.

CAN I USE THIS GUIDE WITH OTHER VERSIONS?

Although this guide uses Microsoft Access 2013, you shouldn't have too much difficulty following the tasks if you have Microsoft Access 2010. The main difference is that two data types, Small Text *and* Long Text, *are called* Text *and* Memo *respectively in Microsoft Access 2010.*

Thanks to:

My wife, as always, for putting up with things. Also, the late Jack Kane from *Record Collector* magazine for, in 2005, asking me about the possibility of writing a series of articles on building a database for storing record collection data. Sadly, Jack died very soon afterwards and the subsequent editor never did answer my emails, so I concluded that the idea too had died.

The idea continued to tumble about in my head, however, and part of what would have made up the first article found itself used instead in a presentation I gave as part of a job application the following year. Waste not, want not. I got the job despite one of the worst interviews I've ever given (I took the phone call offering me the job whilst I was drowning my sorrows in the nearest hospitable real ale pub). I've often wondered how bad the other candidates' interviews must have been.

Anyway, it is nice to think that Jack Kane's idea is commemorated in some way in this book. The record collection database used to describe the niceties of relational database design is very different to the one that would have appeared in *Record Collector*, but the method of describing the development method – branded here as the BATS Technique© – remains from that initial write up of ideas for presenting such a potentially convoluted beast as database development.

INTRODUCTION

Building Relational Databases Made Easy uses Microsoft Access 2013 to show how to build small–scale relational databases. It takes as its starting point the three relational designs developed in the sister book, *Database Design Made Easy*, and works through the first of these – a database to hold record collection data for insurance reasons – with a running commentary on what you are doing and why, all in simple to understand language with all jargon excised (or at least explained).

The two further examples (one small business and one research example), as in the first book, provide the opportunity for further practice and consolidation by letting you get on with the tasks yourself as much as is possible – and if you get stuck, just turn back to the first example to remind yourself of what to do. These two examples introduce a few additional issues, so those particular parts are worked in full the same as with the fully–worked example.

I know what you're thinking. You're thinking that your own database design will not be the same as those covered in this book. Good point, but what this book does is to provide you with the *building blocks* required to build any relational database from a relational design. It doesn't matter if your design has two tables or two hundred tables, what you do is exactly the same as described within. This book had to use some example or other to explain the building blocks, so the examples from *Database Design Made Easy* seemed sensible choices.

We then add a few bells and whilstles – things that are not building blocks for any database, but which will make it easier to use these specific databases and which will give you some idea of what otherwise can be done for your database.

Before we get started, however, it is important to point out that you need to have a relational design ready before you even think about touching any software. Without a valid relational design you will just be wasting your time. The problem is that some software companies tell you that you can just get on and build your database without bothering with any of that relational design malarky. This is basically going to lead either to failure or to building, essentially, a spread sheet in more expensive software. No, you need to design your database first.

This doesn't mean that you need to go away and learn all about relational design, however, because the sister book to this one, *Database Design Made Easy*, introduces a revolutionary, new method – the TONTO Technique© – that does away with the need to understand and use relational theory. Instead it tells you to get drawing (with crayons if you like) because, if you can draw your data entry screen (or screens) on paper, this tells you everything you need to know about the relational design underneath.

If you don't yet have a relational design, then the suggestion is to go and get yourself a copy of *Database Design Made Easy* so that you can come up with your own database design in advance of starting on this book. Once you've got your relational design and your hand–drawn data entry screen design(s), then the suggestion is that you build your own database as you follow the worked example. Or build the worked example and then build your own database. It's up to you!

DATABASE BASICS

At the top level, databases are made up of different things, all of which, in database terms are called *objects*. *Yes, I'm keeping up.* All of these objects are themselves made up of lots of other, for want of a better word, objects (you might also find them termed *controls*, which doesn't generally help). *Ah.* And all of these things have their own set of attributes or properties that define what they do and how they work. *Um.*

Lost yet? Don't worry if you are. We'll work through gently and you'll see what all of this means in real terms. In fact, the best way to get to grips with all of this is to start building the database to see all of this in action. Still, we need to know what these top level objects are and what they do before we jump in and start to build them.

Top level database objects

The first two database objects are *tables* and data entry screens, these latter called *forms* in database–speak because they do the same job as paper forms. The other two objects are *queries* and *reports*.

Macros and *modules* are often described as objects, but these are really commands that (amongst other more esoteric possibilities) do things to or with your data, or to one or more objects. We'll create a couple of macros before we're done, but we won't touch on modules. Modules are for the more overtly heavy tech–heads out there – these basically use code to do snappy things. I've never needed to build one in over twenty years so we'll ignore them. Modules are not for beginners.

If you have already worked through the sister book, *Database Design Made Easy*, then you will already be familiar with the concept of tables and forms, in that you will already have designed one or more data entry screens (forms) on paper and will also have come up with your relational database design. The relational design basically shows you what tables you need to build and what relationships you need to add between those tables.

Tables

Tables effectively *are* your database. This is where the data is stored and all of the other objects do something either with or to this data (well, queries can do other things besides, but we don't really need to know about that).

Tables, however, are not the best objects to use to add, edit or delete your data because, for one thing, you have far too much control over your data; if you decide to delete everything in one go, your database will just let you. As far as the database is concerned it's your data, so you, presumably, know what you want to do with it. This generally leads to tears and finding out, the hard way, about the advisability of creating regular back–ups of your database.

Also, tables show lots of records at the same time, which can be confusing. And it is not unknown to accidentally hit a downward arrow instead of the sideways one and find yourself updating the wrong records.

Forms (data entry screens)

Forms – we'll stop calling them *data entry screens* here and start calling them by their database name – remove much of the danger from databases by letting you see (and so concentrate) on one record at a time. So forms are the best place to add, edit and delete data.

There's one thing that it is very important to know, which is that the form is just another way into the table(s). If you update data in a form, then you have updated that data in the table(s) as well; so if you delete something in the form, then it's gone for good. Shall I mention the need for regular back–ups again?

Queries

Queries, at most basic, let you filter the data in your tables to see just that data you need. So instead of seeing everything at once, you can, for example, choose to see just those people that live in Nempnet Thrubwell (it really exists) or just those birds that breed in saltwater marshes or just those parasites that affect ruminants. Or whatever it is that you keep data about in your database.

Reports

Queries look lousy if you try to print them out – they give you just the data that you need, but in tabular format. Reports let you give context to the data by formatting it in the way that you want and letting you add extra content in a print–friendly style.

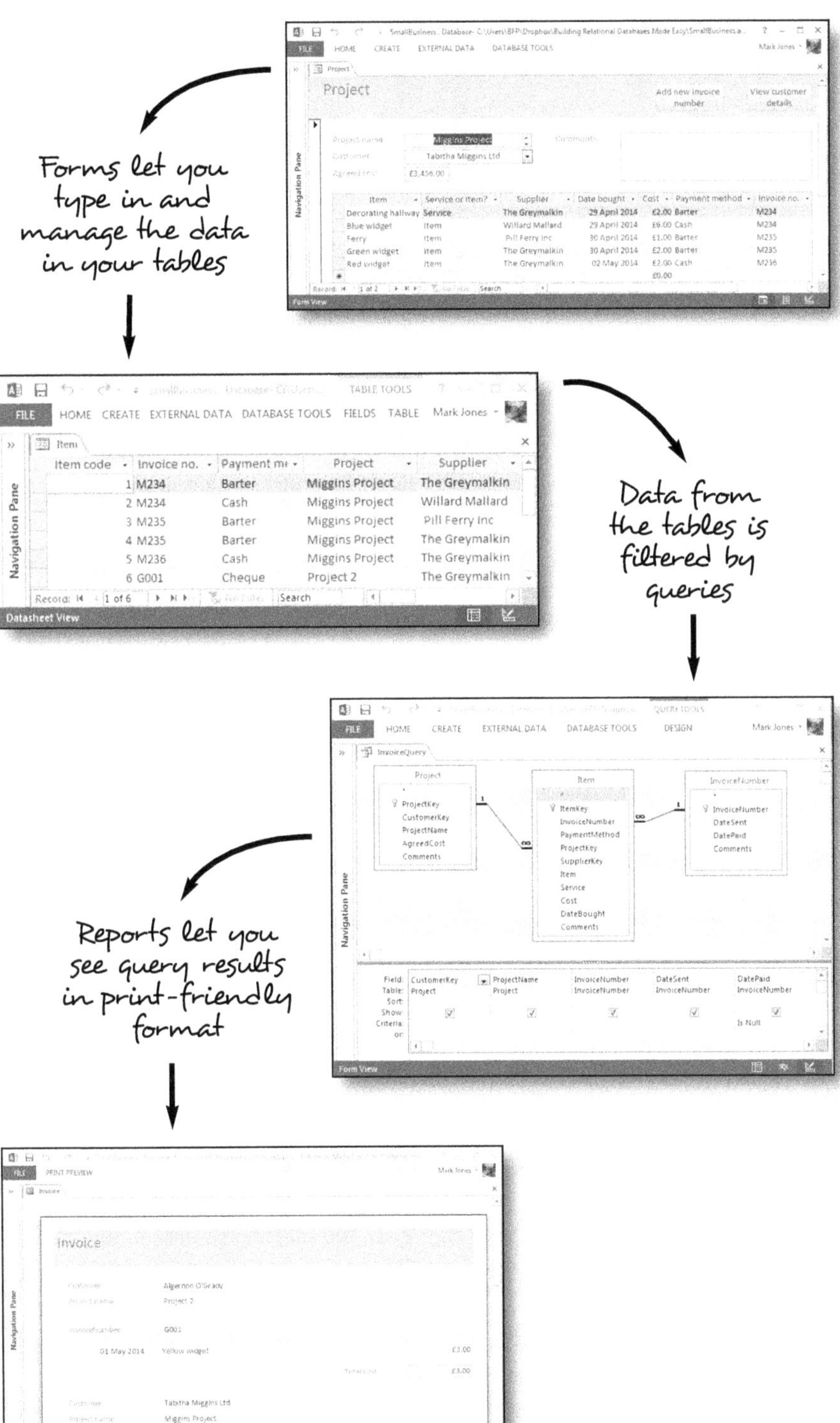

Forms let you type in and manage the data in your tables
Data from the tables is filtered by queries
Reports let you see query results in print-friendly format

THE BUILDING BLOCKS

It doesn't matter which relational database software you intend to use, the building blocks of relational design are always the same. Some software, however, requires you to do things in specific ways – and Microsoft Access 2013 is no exception. Below, then, are the building blocks of relational database design, followed by what this means in terms of using Microsoft Access 2013.

These building blocks are very simple, which is probably why many books, at this point, just start listing everything your chosen software lets you do, rather than making things easy for you and picking out the things that you *have* to do no matter what your database is for.

This book just keeps it simple and ignores all the irrelevant functionality. If you ever want to extend what your database does later on, then that's the time to head off for one of those 'describe–all' books.

There are some other building blocks that come before the building of the database, but you should already have done these. These are the ones included below in italics – and if you haven't done these things yet, then go and do them before you get started with any software. I think I've already mentioned that there's another of my books that takes you through these tasks.

The building blocks of relational database development

These cover only those tasks common to the building of every database and so do not go beyond the development of tables, relationships and forms. Although many databases require the building of queries and reports, these can be viewed as part and parcel of *using* the database, not of *building* it. Even if you have to build them!

Whilst we're at it, purists might say that even the building of data entry forms is going too far and that once you've built the tables and relationships then you've got your database. Technically, the purists are right, but what you have at that point is not particularly usable as a database, especially for those not used to working with tables. So, whether rightly or wrongly – it goes without saying that I think that I'm right, of course – we cover the building of forms here.

What you should already have done

i. Designed your data entry screen(s) using pen and paper, paying particlular attention to where you want to choose data from a drop–down and where you want to type data into a list.

ii. Used the other steps in the TONTO Technique© to come up with your relational design.

iii. Decided on data types for every data entry field, assigned field size and/or format and given all tables and fields acceptable names.

What you still have to do – introducing the BATS Technique©

1. *B*uild your tables.
2. *A*dd the relationships.
3. *T*est your database.
4. *S*et up the data entry form(s).

The building blocks using Microsoft Access 2013

There are no prizes for guessing that moving on to working through the above four building blocks in real terms using Microsoft Access 2013 (or, indeed, any relational database software) means a lot of extra detail to think about. The following provides some general advice on each building block followed by a detailed list of Microsoft Access 2013–specific steps.

Build your tables

This is a wonderfully straightforward task, if usually somewhat monotonous after the second table, and requires you to convert your *relational design* into Microsoft Access 2013 tables, prior to adding relationships. Don't be tempted to drift off into sleep mode because it really *does* matter what data types you select and the sizes and/or formats you assign to your data entry fields. Before you start might be a good time to make yourself a very large mug of coffee.

The relational design, for those who still haven't worked through *Database Design Made Easy*, despite all the heavy–handed hints, consists of the drawing showing all required tables and relationships, which you come up with at the end of Step 4 of the TONTO Technique©, and the list of tables, fields and so on that you come up with at the end of Step 7. At least, that will be *came up with* for those that have already worked through that book.

With Microsoft Access 2013 you need, for each table, to:

1. Create each individual data entry field.
2. Assign data type and specify the size/format for each data entry field.
3. Create captions for any data entry fields with 'inelegant' names; for example, Microsoft Access 2013 can show the field name for *CatalogueNumber* as *Cat. no.* if we like (we just have to remember that in the backgound it is still really called *CatalogueNumber*).
4. Add any required properties, such as default values if a field is generally going to include the same piece of data; for example, most records in the *Record* table are from the UK, so we can make our database enter *UK* automatically for each new record.
5. Assign the primary key and ensure that all foreign keys are present and set to the correct data entry type, size and/or format.
6. Save and name the table.

CAN I PUT SOME DATA IN NOW?

No! *Do not be tempted to type any data into your tables until building block 3 or, most likely, you'll never get through building block 2. A cardinal rule is never to add data until after you have created* all *required relationships.*

Add the relationships

There are some things that you need to know about relationships, these things relating to such beasts as *referential integrity*, *cascade update* and *cascade delete*. We won't talk about them just yet, but will return to them later when we start building the database. In the meantime, beware of any options that include the word *delete* (and, as from Microsoft Access 2013, any that include the words *multiple values*).

With Microsoft Access 2013 you need to:

1. For all tables where where you have a foreign key, make every foreign key into a look–up, assigning referential integrity in each instance (this 'half' builds relationships between the main table and the look–up tables); bear in mind the next point, below, during this part.
2. Where a drop–down (which is what a look–up creates) needs to contain data from more than one field, or descriptive text instead of code or auto number, set the drop–down to display the required data.
3. Complete all of the half–finished look–ups in the *Relationships window*.

Test your database

This is the task that many database development books forget to tell you about, often because they don't really tell you how to build a database but instead just describe all the software features. The reality is that this is the point at which you find out if you got your relational design right or not.

Let's put it this way, if you lost concentration for a while during *Database Design Made Easy* (it is somewhat soporific in places, I know) and put the *1*s and *M*s at the wrong ends of one or more lines, then you will end up with drop–downs where you wanted sub–forms and vice versa. If this happens, then you will have to go back and have a good look at your relational design. It generally means, in real terms, having to do some piggery jokery with foreign keys (deleting the wrong 'foreign key' from one end of the relationship and adding the correct foreign key at the other). At worst, this might mean having to go right through the whole TONTO Technique© again, but this shouldn't take you too long, so it's not the end of the world. Just stay alert this time, that's all.

With Microsoft Access 2013 you need to:

1. Enter a small amount of test data into each of the look–up tables (i.e. the tables that feed drop–downs).
2. Enter a couple of records into your main table, choosing data from drop–downs.
3. Check the data in any sub–tables.
4. If you have a sub–table where you expected a drop–down, or vice versa, then repair work is in order.

Set up the data entry form(s)

This can be as straightforward or as difficult as you like. If you are happy with the form as automatically created (with some input from you) by Microsoft Access 2013, then only minor work will be needed.

If, however, you want the form to look *exactly* like your paper design, and won't be happy until it does, then there may be the need for some fiddly work afoot. That, of course, is up to you, but bear in mind that this book doesn't dwell much on making your form look pretty. It's more interested in getting you to the point at which you have a working database.

With Microsoft Access 2013 you need to:

1. Create each required data entry form using the *Form Wizard* option, which, if necessary, lets you create sub–forms automatically.
2. If you need more than one sub–form in any one form, you have to create these separately and then add them to your main form.
3. Make any minor changes (or major ones if you really want to) to the formatting so as to allow ease of use during data entry.
4. Save each form as you go or you may lose some of your changes if things go horribly wrong (as they sometimes can with formatting tasks).

ADDITIONAL TASKS

There are two parts to this:

1. Those things that your database needs to do so as to be of use to you.
2. Those things that can make the everyday use of your database easier – in other words, 'bells and whistles'.

Two of the three example scenarios include information about how the database needs to work, whilst the first example suggests at least one calculation, not overtly mentioned, that might be required if the database is to be used for the stated purpose, which is that of coming up with an overall value for insurance purposes.

Even though you most likely won't be doing these specific things with your own particular database, these will at least show you some of the possibilities, which, in turn, may spark some ideas for making your database even more useful.

It's always a good idea, not just to revisit the stated scenarios, but also to think around the reason for the database's existence. This often suggests one or more requirements for further functionality.

Other tasks, such as adding navigation buttons, are not essential to the building of every database, but are what make databases easy to use. These tasks, although they do not come within the remit of the stated building blocks, are included in this guide because these are commonly–required tasks that it is good to know about.

FULLY WORKED EXAMPLE

The starting point here is the relational design and the hand–drawn data entry form that you came up with using the sister book to this, *Database Development Made Easy*. The relational design is in two parts, remember; these are the drawing showing all required tables and relationships, which you come up with at the end of Step 4 of the TONTO Technique©, and the list of tables, fields and so on that you come up with at the end of Step 7.

You also need to refer to the scenario. Now that you've moved on from the design to the development stage, it's amazing what you notice is missing. Yes, in the real world, this is often the point at which things that you've forgotton to mention come to light. If it's just a case of adding in the odd data entry field, then this shouldn't cause too many problems. Though do bear in mind that if any of those fields suggest a drop–down or a sub–form, then you will have further tables on your hands and may have to go back to the TONTO Technique© to remind yourself how to add new tables and relationships to your design.

The building blocks are exactly the same no matter what relational design you have. You will build tables for your own database in exactly the same way as seen here. The same is true for all the other objects – the process remains the same, just the individual options chosen as you go through each block may be different.

There is one very important thing to understand about building your database, and that is that there are two distinct views (more, but we'll come to these later). One is the design view, where you build and modify each object, and the other is the normal view, where you then use the object. We'll spend most, but not all, of our time in design view of one object or another.

The example scenario and the relational design are as follows:

> *I need to keep a record of my music collection for insurance purposes. I want to keep a record of every artist in my collection, along with a list of every record I have by them, whatever the format – LP, CD, cassette, 7" single, one–off track digital download, flexi disc, etc. So that I can assign the correct value to each individual record, I need to be able to record the catalogue number, format, record label, label design and condition, plus any additional information that might affect value. I also want to know when I bought the record and how much it cost me. It would be quite nice to assign each artist with a genre too, if that's not too difficult.*

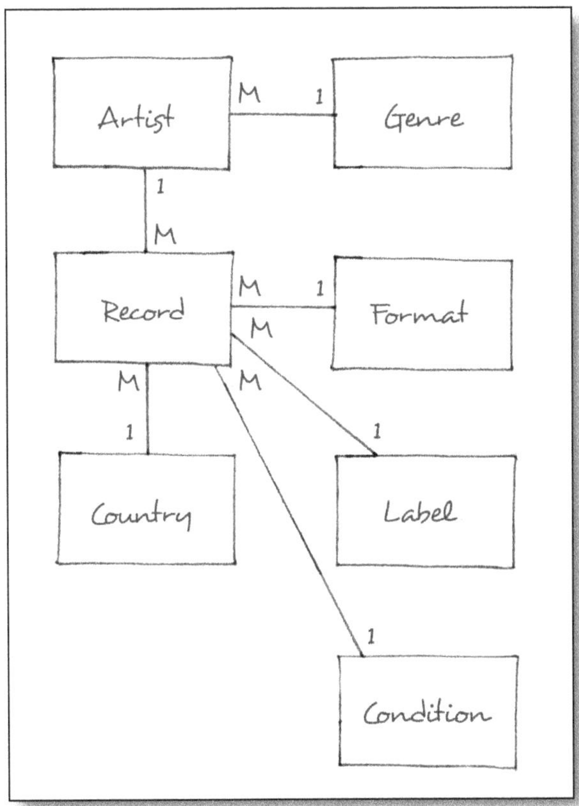

Figure 1. The relational design for the record collection database showing all identified tables along with the relationships between those tables.

Table	Field name (key)	Data type	Size/format
Artist	ArtistKey (PK)	Auto number	–
	Genre (FK)	Short Text	30
	ArtistName1	Short Text	100
	ArtistName2	Short Text	100
	Comments	Long Text	–
Condition	Condition (PK)	Short Text	20
	Comments	Long Text	–
Country	Country (PK)	Short Text	50
	Comments	Long Text	–
Format	Format (PK)	Short Text	30
	Comments	Long Text	–
Genre	Genre (PK)	Short Text	30
	Comments	Long Text	–
Label	Label (PK)	Short Text	100
	Comments	Long Text	–
Record	RecordKey (PK)	Auto number	–
	ArtistKey (FK)	Number	Long Integer
	Condition (FK)	Short Text	20
	Country (FK)	Short Text	50
	Format (FK)	Short Text	30
	Label (FK)	Short Text	100
	Title	Short Text	255
	CatalogueNumber	Short Text	30
	Cost	Currency	£
	Value	Currency	£
	DateBought	Date/Time	Long Date
	Comments	Long Text	–

Table 1. Record collection database tables, fields and properties with database–friendly names.

Build your tables

Creating a new database

To create a new database:

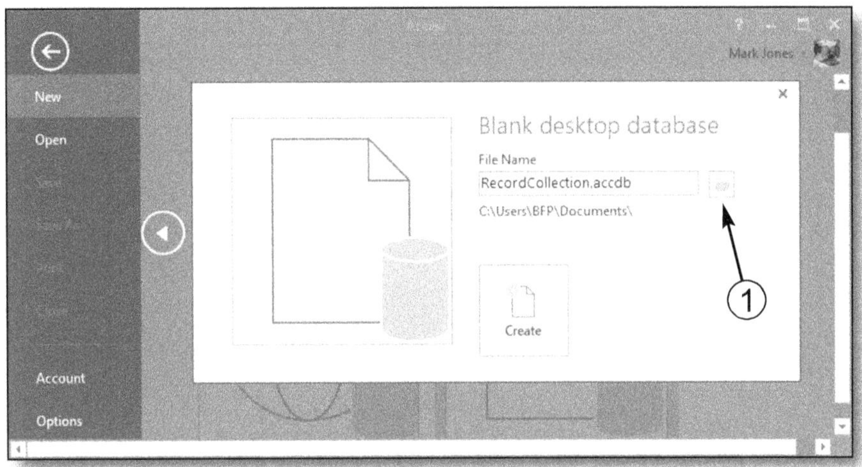

1. Open Microsoft Access 2013 and select *Blank desktop database*.
2. In *File Name* give the database a sensible name – in this instance we'll call it **RecordCollection** (Microsoft Access 2013 adds the *.accdb* suffix even if you overwrite it).
3. Click on the file icon (1) and select where you want to save the database.
4. Click on *Create*, which opens the new database.
5. We do not want to start adding data into the table that Microsoft Access 2013 has 'helpfully' opened, so close it by right–clicking on the tab that says *Table1* and choosing *Close*.

The work environment

In Microsoft Access 2013 you use the same space to build your objects as you do to use them when the database is finished. The *Ribbon* has contextualised commands, so you you will see different options depending on what you are doing.

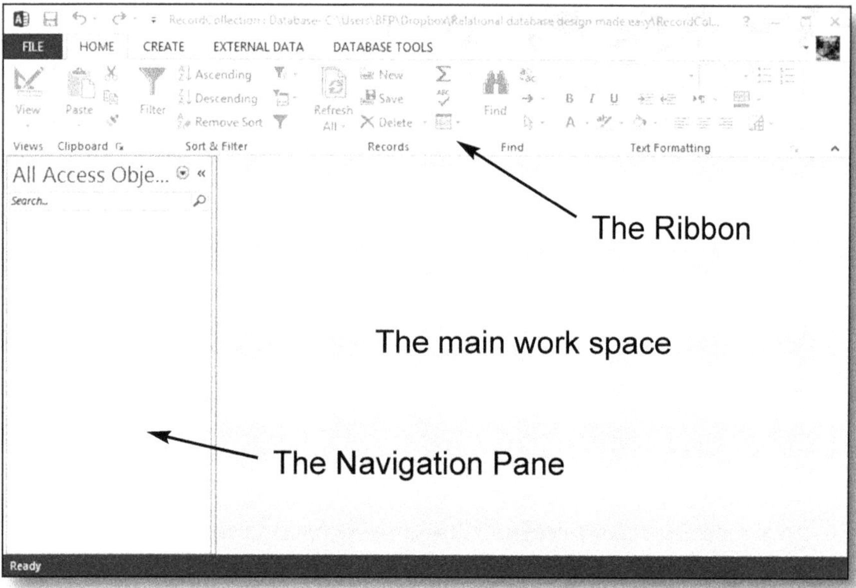

You build each object in the main work space. When you save an object it appears in the *Navigation Pane*, from which you can open objects to use them by double–clicking on them (right–clicking from here lets you open them in design view).

Two important points:

> **1.** If you open your database and there is a yellow bar across the top of the work space, under the *Ribbon*, click the button that says *Enable*. If you don't do this it disappears eventually, but various things won't work. If you forget, just close the database and open it again, this time selecting *Enable*. This only goes for your own database – bear in mind that this is a security warning; databases from other sources could hold malicious code that could kill your computer or disclose your passwords.
>
> **2.** Never have more than one object open at the same time if you are building or modifying an object. If you do this, it is possible that Microsoft Access 2013 will refuse to save your work. You have been warned.

Building your first table

Field name (key)	Data type	Size/format	Caption
RecordKey (PK)	Auto number	—	Record code
ArtistKey (FK)	Number	Long Integer	Artist code
Condition (FK)	Short Text	20	—
Country (FK)	Short Text	50	—
Format (FK)	Short Text	30	—
Label (FK)	Short Text	100	—
Title	Short Text	255	—
CatalogueNumber	Short Text	30	Cat. no.
Cost	Currency	£	—
Value	Currency	£	—
DateBought	Date/Time	Long Date	Date bought
Comments	Long Text	—	—

Table 2. The *Record* table including suggestions for captions for those less user–friendly field names.

To create the first table (we'll start with the *Record* table because it has the most data entry fields and provides the most variety):

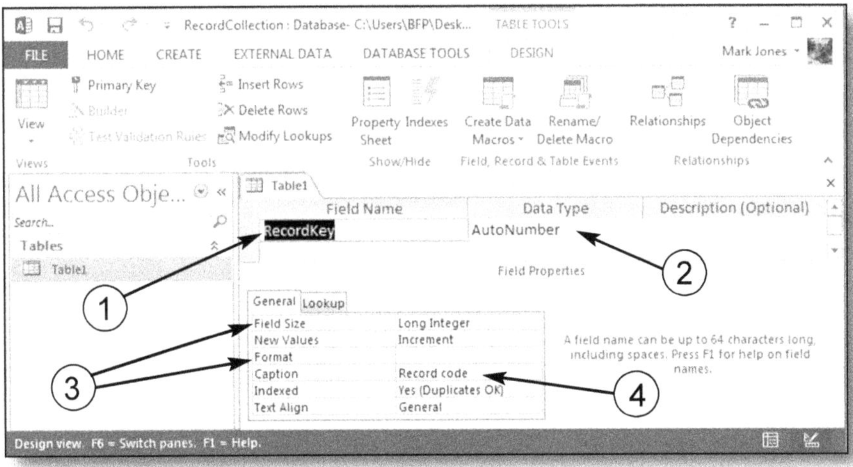

1. Click on the *Create* tab above the *Ribbon* and select *Table Design*.
2. This may sound obvious, but type the field name from the above table into the *Field Name* column (1) – don't type in *(PK)* or *(FK)*, these are just there to remind you that these are keys – then click in the *Data Type*

column and select the relevant data type from the drop–down (2); then update either field size or format in the *Field Size* or *Format* fields in the *Field Properties* section (3) – note that for formats, you should click in the *Format* field and select the relevant format from the drop–down that appears; finally, add any required captions in the *Caption* field (4).

WHAT IF I GET IT WRONG?

Troubleshooting can be the stuff of nightmares. Do spend the time to double–check everything when it comes to data types, field sizes and/or formats, especially for any fields that will be primary or foreign keys – and we have quite a few foreign keys in this table.

If you need to amend the design of a table once saved and closed, right–click on it in the Navigation Pane *and select* Design View.

To define the primary key, fine tune and save the table:

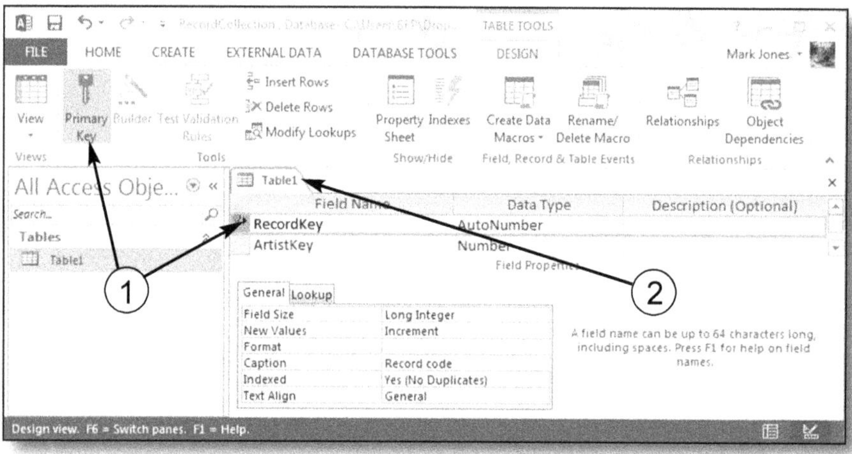

1. Click in the *RecordKey* row and click the *Primary Key* icon (1).
2. Click in *Country* and, in *Default Value* (in *Field Properties)*, type in **UK** – this will now be entered automatically every time you add a new record.
3. Right–click on the table tab (2), select *Close* from the pop–up menu, say *Yes* to saving changes and call the table **Record**. Notice that your new table now appears in the *Navigation Pane*, where you can double–click on it to open it.
5. If you open the table DO NOT be tempted to type in any data yet.

Building the other six tables

To do this, just follow the guidelines for building the *Record* table but using the field names, data types, field sizes/formats and captions from the following tables. Don't forget to define the primary keys for each table and DO NOT enter any data in any table, no matter how BIG the temptation.

Field name (key)	Data type	Size/format	Caption
ArtistKey (PK)	Auto number	—	Artist code
Genre (FK)	Short Text	30	—
ArtistName1	Short Text	100	First name/The
ArtistName2	Short Text	100	Surname/Band name
Comments	Long Text	—	—

Table 3. The *Artist* table.

Field name (key)	Data type	Size/format	Caption
Condition (PK)	Short Text	20	—
Comments	Long Text	—	—

Table 4. The *Condition* table.

Field name (key)	Data type	Size/format	Caption
Country (PK)	Short Text	50	—
Comments	Long Text	—	—

Table 5. The *Country* table.

Field name (key)	Data type	Size/format	Caption
Format (PK)	Short Text	30	—
Comments	Long Text	—	—

Table 6. The *Format* table.

Field name (key)	Data type	Size/format	Caption
Genre (PK)	Short Text	30	—
Comments	Long Text	—	—

Table 7. The *Genre* table.

Field name (key)	Data type	Size/format	Caption
Label (PK)	Short Text	100	—
Comments	Long Text	—	—

Table 8. The *Label* table.

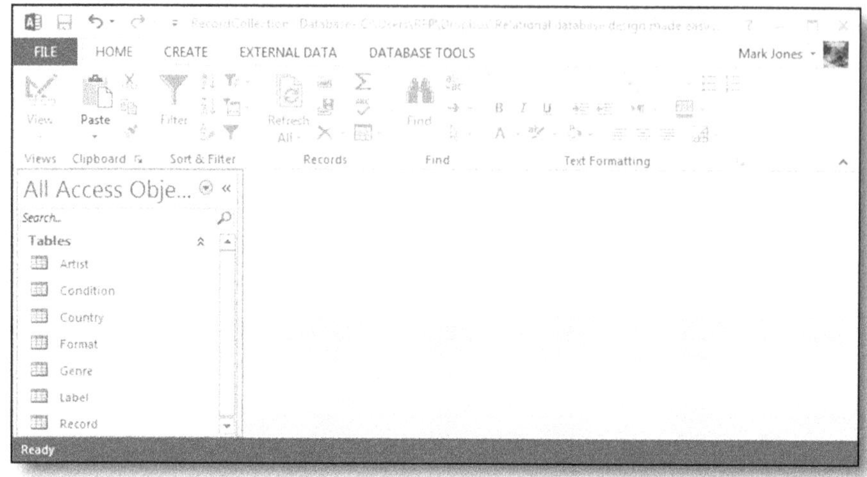

You should now have seven tables showing in the Navigation Pane. If your database doesn't look like the above screenshot, then go back and see which table(s) you've forgotten to build.

Now, I know I'm nagging, but you weren't tempted to put any data into any of the tables, were you? Good, in that case the next building block should be easy. If you put data into tables before you have created the relationships, then it is highly likely that you will fall foul of referential integrity rules.

Don't worry, you'll find out soon what *referential integrity* means. Suffice to say, for the moment, that it's what makes relational databases work – or, at least, what makes them work without duplicating data. And if you're happy to duplicate (and potentially lose) data, then you might as well stick with a spread sheet. For more on this, see the sister book, *Database Design Made Easy*.

Add the relationships

Creating look–ups for drop–downs

The above sounds topsy–turvy, I know, but in every instance where you want to choose data from a drop–down you need to create a look–up to the table in which the data for the drop–down is stored. Once you've done this, the drop–downs will automatically appear when you later build the data entry forms (otherwise you would have to create all look–ups one at a time and 'manually', which is not fun to do).

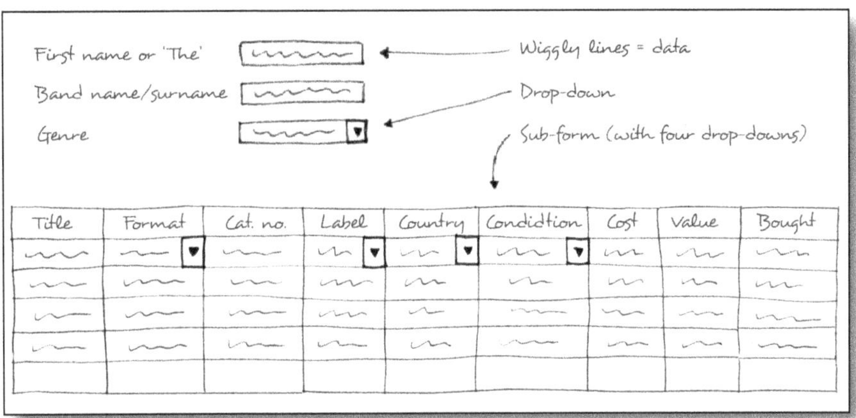

Above is the hand–drawn design for this current database, which shows where the designer wants to choose data from drop–downs; there are five drop–downs, one in the *Artist* table (the table that data is fed into from the main form) and four in the *Record* table (the table that data is fed into from the sub–form).

You need to create look–ups for the following fields:

- In the *Record* table you need look–ups for the *Condition*, *Country*, *Format* and *Label* fields.
- In the *Artist* table you need a look–up for the *Genre* field.

Again, we'll work through one example together and then I'll leave you to create the rest on your own. If you can build one look–up, then you can build almost every look–up. The exceptions are where you want to view more than one field in a drop–down (such as someone's name) and/or where the foriegn key (it is not coincidental that all of the above drop–downs happen to be foreign keys) shows a code or autonumber. In this instance you will probably want to view a different piece of data, such as viewing a widget's name instead of its reorder number.

WHAT IF MY OWN DATABASE HAS THESE EXCEPTIONS?

You can see how to handle these exceptions by referring to the two additional examples. Both the small business and research examples include the above two exceptions combined.

You have to create the look–ups before you create the relationships – at least, the creation of each look–up partially creates the relationship, but does not complete it. Therefore, once you've created the look–ups, you then need to complete the relationships. Then you need to set up any remaining relationships. Refer back to the relational design on page 15 – the design is the overall blueprint for the database, so you need to make sure that, by the end of this building block, all of the identified relationships have been created.

To create a look–up for the *Genre* field in the *Artist* table:

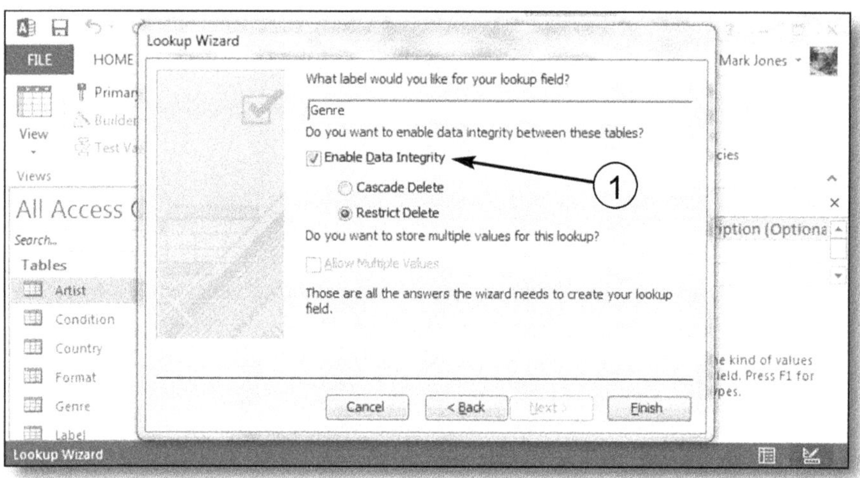

1. Right–click on the *Artist* table in the *Navigation Pane* and select *Design View* from the pop–up menu.
2. Click in the *Data Type* field for *Genre* and select *Lookup Wizard...* from the drop–down that appears.
3. Click on *Next* in the pop–up wizard, choose *Table: Genre* from the next screen and click *Next.*
4. In *Available Fields*, double–click on *Genre* to move it to *Selected Fields* and click *Next.*
5. Sort by *Genre*, ascending, click *Next* and *Next* again.
6. Tick the *Enable Data Integrity* box (1) – do not select anything else here – and click on *Finish*; save the table when prompted.

To test the new look–up:

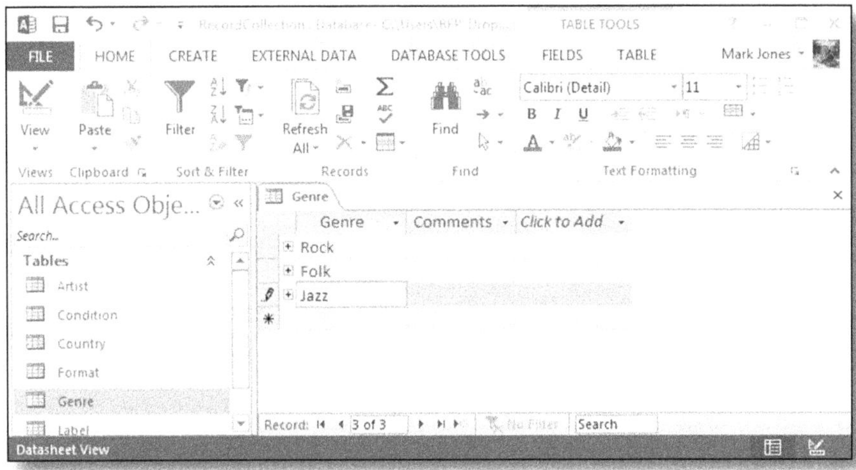

1. Close the table by right–clicking on the *Artist* tab above the table and selecting *Close*. (Close all objects this way from here on.)
2. Open the *Genre* table from the *Navigation Pane* by double–clicking it. (Open all objects this way from now on, unless opening in design view.)
3. In the *Genre* field type in **Rock** in the first record, then directly below in the second record type **Folk**; add **Jazz** as the third record. (Don't add anything to the *Comments* field.)
4. Close the *Genre* table and open the *Artist* table.
5. Press the *Tab* key on the keyboard to tab across to the *Genre* field and notice that a drop–down appears. Press the *F4* key to show the drop–down options – though don't select any of the options yet.
6. Close the *Artist* table. If you accidentally added a genre to the field, then you will need to press the *Esc* key either once or twice to undo your data entry before you can close the table.

Yes, I know that I've just broken my own rule about not putting in any data until Block 3, but we can cheat a bit here because we've already partially created the relationship between these two particular tables.

When it comes down to it, it is a case of do as I say and not as I do, at least until such time as you know what you're doing well enough to know when you can safely break the rules!

To create look–ups for the four drop–downs in the *Record* table:

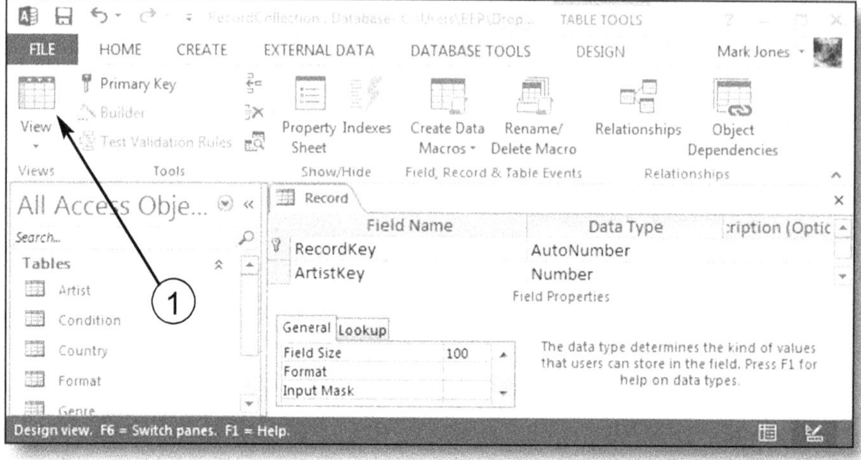

1. Make sure that all tables are closed, right–click on the *Record* table in the *Navigation Pane* and select *Design View.* (Open all objects in design view this way from here on, unless suggested otherwise.)

2. Do exactly the same as you did for the *Genre* field in the *Artist* table, only this time for the *Condition* field (the table you want to look up is, oddly enough, *Table: Condition*), saving when prompted.

3. Do the same as above for *Country*, *Format* and *Label* (looking up, respectively, *Table: Country*, *Table: Format* and *Table: Label*).

4. Click on the *View* icon (1) to view the *Record* table with the recent changes and tab through the fields to see where the drop–downs appear – note that there is no data to choose from these drop–downs yet, but we'll test this during the next building block – then close the table.

I KEEP GETTING AN ERROR MESSAGE

If you get an error message along the lines of Record has changed since last time you opened it... *just click* OK. *This often means that you are trying to build or make changes to an object whilst another object is open. Microsoft Access 2013 really doesn't like that. Sometimes the message pops up even with all other objects closed, in which case it might be time to close the application down and reopen it. The worst that can happen is that it won't save the last thing you did, so you may have to redo it – this only relates to development work rather than typing in data.*

Completing the look-up relationships

As already mentioned, creating a look–up half builds the relationship between the table with the drop–down and the table from which you need to choose the data for the drop–down. Quite why you can't complete the relationship whilst building the look–up is a good question. You just can't, that's all.

To complete the look–up relationships:

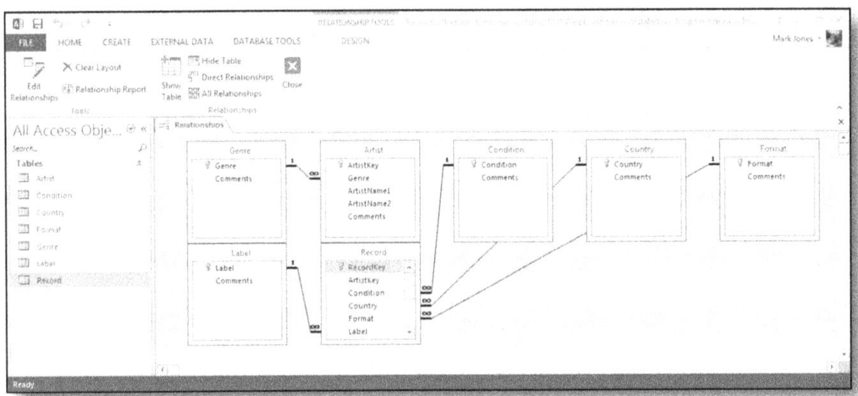

1. Make sure that all tables are closed (never leave any objects open if trying to do any development work in Microsoft Access 2013.) then click on the *Database Tools* tab above the *Ribbon* and select *Relationships*.

2. In the *Relationships* window, depending on your set–up, you may see two, seven or no tables! If you can see seven tables, then all is well; if not, click on the *Show Table* icon in the *Ribbon* and double–click on every table that isn't already showing to add it to the window so that you have something like the above screenshot (the tables might be in a different order). You should see one relationship (i.e. line between tables) for every look–up you created. If any are missing, then close the *Relationships* window (saving changes, if prompted) and go and create the look–up before retrying this task.

3. This is fiddly, but right–click on the thin part of the relationship line between *Genre* and *Artist* (i.e. not at either end, where the line is thicker) and then select *Edit Relationship...* from the pop–up menu (if you don't get this option, then you missed the line – I did say this was fiddly – so try again).

4. In the new window, select *Cascade Update Related Records* (1). If *Enforce Referential Integrity* is unticked, then tick this as well – you should already have chosen this when creating the look–up so, if it is unticked, pay more attention!

5. Leave *Cascade Delete Related Records* unticked – ticking this can have dreadful consequences for your data later on – and click on *OK.*

6. Do exactly the same for the other four relationships.

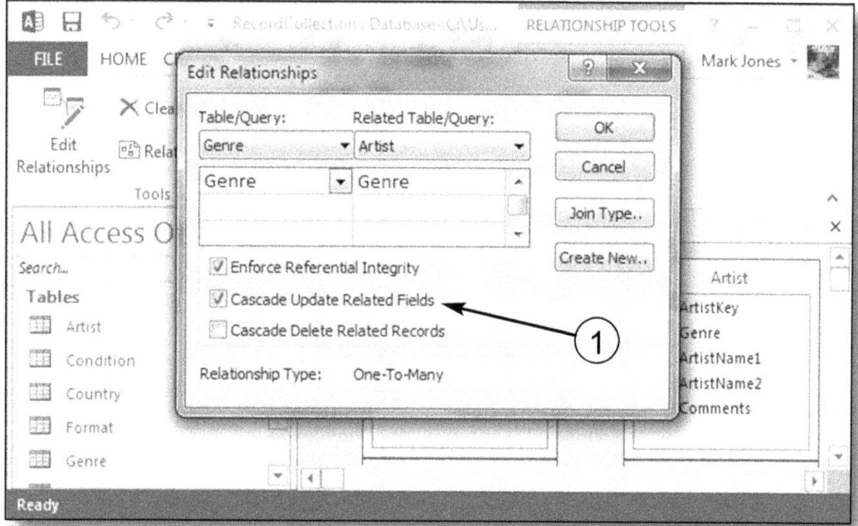

WHAT IS REFERENTIAL INTEGRITY?

Referential integrity is what relational databases work upon. In basic terms, if you don't have something in a drop–down list, then you can't add it to the record you're updating. If you need to add it to the record, then you have to add it to the list first (i.e. by adding it to the table that the drop–down looks up) and then it is available for use and reuse from the drop–down.

WHAT ABOUT THE TWO 'CASCADE' OPTIONS?

Cascade update is good. It means that if you, for example, mis–spell a genre, such as Ruck 'n' mole *instead of* Rock 'n' roll, *you can correct it in the* Genre *table and Microsoft Access 2013 will automatically update the old version of that data in every* Artist *record in which it is used. So you don't have to go and look for every instance and manually update it.*

Cascade delete, on the other hand, has its uses but is generally bad. For example, if you have this option ticked and you accidentally delete an artist record in the Artist *table, Microsoft Access 2013 will automatically delete every record by that artist in the* Record *table as well as deleting the artist record. With the option unticked, you cannot accidentally delete any record from one table where there are related records in another table. Guess how I found this out.*

Adding any missing relationships

If we compare the relational design on p. 15 with what we have in the *Relationships* window we can see if we are still missing one or more relationship. To make things easier, you can drag the various tables around, so that they are in the same place in the *Relationships* window as they are in the relational design.

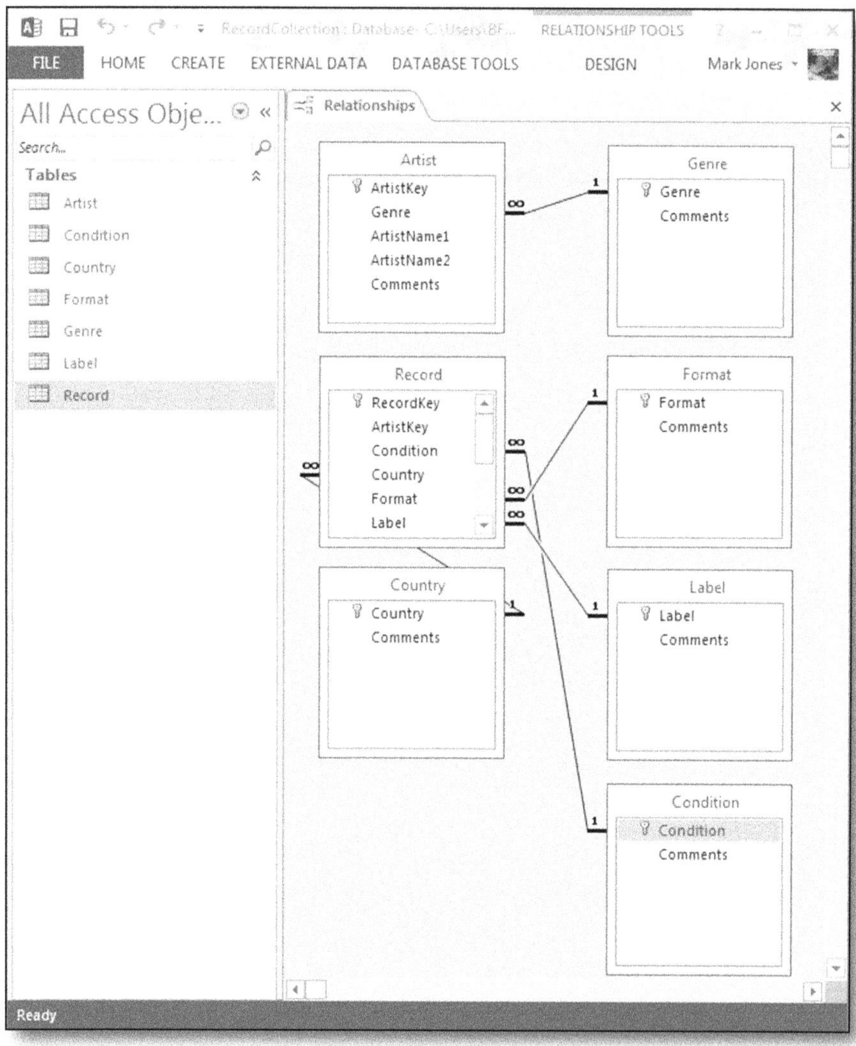

We can see from the screenshot that we are still missing the relationship between the *Artist* and *Record* tables. This is because we couldn't see this as a drop–down on the hand–drawn data entry screen. This is the link instead between main form and the sub–form.

We could set the relationship up in the *Relationships* window without creating a look–up first, but this could cause problems later on if we wanted to create another form for entering data about records, from which we would want to choose the artist from a drop–down. Creating the relationship in the *Relationships* window would mean that there would not automatically be a drop–down when we created that form. Worse, we would have to delete the pre–existing relationship before we could create a look–up, should we want one later on. This is fiddly.

So even though we don't necessarily need a look–up at this particular moment, we'll create the relationship between *Artist* and *Record* in exactly the same way as we have with the other relationships.

To add the relationship between *Artist* and *Record*:

1. Open the *Record* table in design view and click in the *Data Type* field for *ArtistKey*, then select *Lookup Wizard...* from the drop–down and do the same as with the other examples, though choosing *Table: Artist* and *ArtistKey* at the relevant points.
2. Do exactly the same as with the other look–ups/relationaships

When we add some test data in the next building block, we will only see the auto number in the *ArtistKey* drop–down. It would be better to see the artist name, but because we're not going to actively use this drop–down we won't worry about that for now. If we ever needed to build the above conjectural form, we could sort this out later. Both the small business and research examples show you how you would get the drop–down to show the two fields that make up a name.

Test your database

Lots of books on database development hardly touch on the extremely important task of testing your database at all. Perhaps this is why so many databases that I've seen in the course of various day jobs have, to a greater or lesser extent, not worked. In fact I'll go so far as to say that over 95% of all the databases I've been asked to look at have been so poorly 'designed' that the owner might as well not have bothered.

Is this the fault of the people building the databases? In my opinion it is not. Until the introduction of the TONTO Technique©, normal, non–techie people, if needing a database, had no alternative but to attempt to understand and use relational design methods – or in most cases, have just tried to get by with no understanding of either the theory or of how unforgiving relational database software is of not getting it right.

Testing your database structure before starting on the time–consuming tasks of building data entry forms and getting your data in has always seemed a sensible approach to me. You might as well find out if you've got something wrong now as opposed to another forty or so hours of effort further on.

Adding test data to look–up tables

The reason for adding test data to the look–up tables first is for the sensible reason that if you've got nothing in a look–up table, then you won't have anything to choose from the drop–down that looks up that table.

We've already added some data to the *Genre* table, but let's add some more. Let's also add some data to the other look–up tables. Enter the data in the table opposite to the tables and fields as indicated.

When we built the *Record* table we added 'UK' as the default value in the *Country* field. If we don't add 'UK' as one of the fields in the *Country* table, we will have some real difficulties later.

Think back to referential integrity – you can only add a piece of data into a look–up field if it exists in the drop–down list; in other words it has to be in the table that the look–up looks up.

Table	Field	Data for entry
Genre	Genre	1960s pop
		Rock 'n' roll
		Hip hop
Format	Format	LP
		CD
		7" single
		12" single
		Cassette
		8-track
		Download, single track
		Download, album
Label	Label	Harvest
		Charisma
		B&C
		Island
		Immediate
		Saydisc
		Village Thing
Condition	Condition	As new
		Excellent
		Very good
		Good
		Fair
Country	Country	UK
		US
		Germany
		Italy

Table 9. Data to enter into the look–up tables as indicated.

Adding test data to the main table

Enter the data below into the *Artist* table. In the table you see the captions that you added when building that table, not the names you gave to the fields (*ArtistName1* has the caption *First name/The* and *ArtistName2* the caption *Surname/Band name*). You cannot type anything into *ArtistKey* (*Artist code* as per caption) because this is an auto number field, where the data is added automatically.

Artistname1	ArtistName2	Genre
The	Beatles	1960s pop
	King Crimson	Rock
Kevin	Ayers	Rock
Captain	Beefheart	Rock
The	Nice	Rock
Dave	Evans	Folk
Fred	Wedlock	Folk

Table 10. Data to enter into the *Artist* table.

Your table should look like the following screenshot.

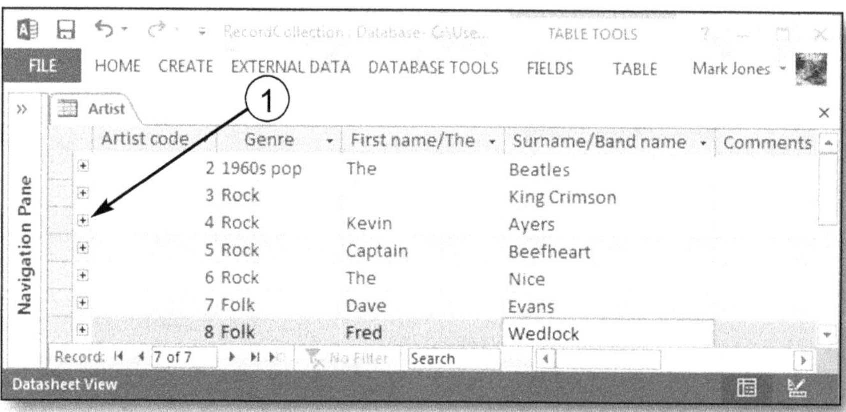

Adding test data to the sub–table

Sub–tables are like sub–forms, only accessible from the table, which means that you can, if you like, manage your data from the table without having to use forms.

However, as already mentioned, tables are not the best places to do the data entry and other data management tasks. Also, sub–tables are not as user–friendly as sub–forms. Sub–tables, indeed all tables, show you all the fields, even those, such as auto number fields, where you can't actually change the data.

You have also probably noticed that the fields are not necessarily in the order in which you will want to enter the data (for example, in *Artist*, *Genre* comes before the artist name fields). We can move things around in the table, but it's much easier to reorder things the way we want on the data entry form when we build it.

To add test data to the *Record* sub–table:

1. In the *Artist* table, click on the small box with plus sign (1) to the left of *Artist code* in the record for *Kevin Ayers*.
2. In the sub–table that opens, enter the data from the table below; click in the *Condition* field and use the drop–down to select the required data, then do the same for *Country*, *Format* and *Label* – just make some data up for the currency and date fields.

Condition	Country	Format	Label	Title	Cat. No.
As new	UK	LP	Harvest	Odd Ditties	SHSM 2005
Excellent	UK	LP	Island	Sweet Deceiver	ILPS 9322
As new	UK	CD	Harvest	Joy of a Toy	07243-582776-2-3

Table 11. Data to enter into the *Record* sub–table.

If you can open the sub–table from within the *Artist* table, and if all of the drop–downs work in both the *Artist* table and the sub–table, then it looks as though you have a working database.

WHAT IF SOMETHING DIDN'T WORK?

If you can't open the sub–table, then you've probably forgotten to add the relationship between the Artist *and* Record *tables. Missing drop–downs probably mean that you missed a look–up. Go back and see what you've done/not done. At the very worst, start again from scratch and follow the instructions more closely second time around – I think that I've already mentioned that relational database software is not tolerant of mistakes.*

Set up the data entry forms

Creating a form with sub-form

We're going to create a data entry form to do exactly the same as we've done with the test data. We want a form to enter artist details and we want, in that form, to be able to type in a list of all the records by a particular artist.

With forms, we can hide all of those fields that we either don't want or need to see, such as auto number key fields. Also, we can set the form so as to have the fields in the order in which we want to type in the data. As we'll see in the following section, we can also add some bells and whistles to make the database easier to use.

There's nothing to stop us from creating data entry forms for the various look–up tables as well as for the main tables. However, look–up tables, especially if there are only one or two fields in the table, can generally be left as they are. In fact, leaving them as tables is generally a good idea because we tend to need to see multiple records at the same time in these tables, so as not to accidentally try to add the same record twice (not that referential integrity would let us, in any case).

To create the main data entry form with sub–form:

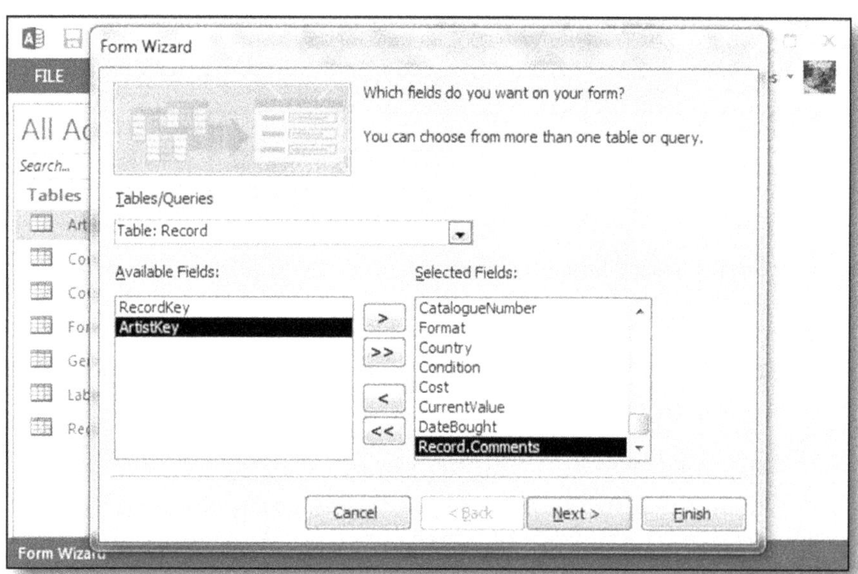

1. Make sure that all the tables are closed and click on the *Create* tab above the *Ribbon*.

2. Select *Form Wizard* from the *Forms* section of the *Ribbon* and from the *Tables/Queries* drop–down select *Table: Artist.*
3. In *Available Fields*, double–click in turn (and in this order) on *ArtistName1*, *ArtistName2*, *Genre* and *Comments* to move them to the *Selected Fields* section.
4. Now select *Table: Record* from the *Tables/Queries* drop–down and move across (again in this order) *Title*, *Label*, *CatalogueNumber*, *Format*, *Country*, *Condition*, *Cost*, *CurrentValue*, *DateBought* and *Comments*, then click on *Next*, followed by *Next* again and *Next* yet again for a third time.
5. Name the form as **ArtistForm** and the sub–form as **RecordSubform**, then click on *Finish*.
6. Type in some records in the sub–form for *The Beatles*, then click on the *Next Record* navigation button (1) at the bottom of the form until you reach the record for *Kevin Ayers* so as to see the data you've already entered via the table. In fact, try all five navigation buttons to see what they do.

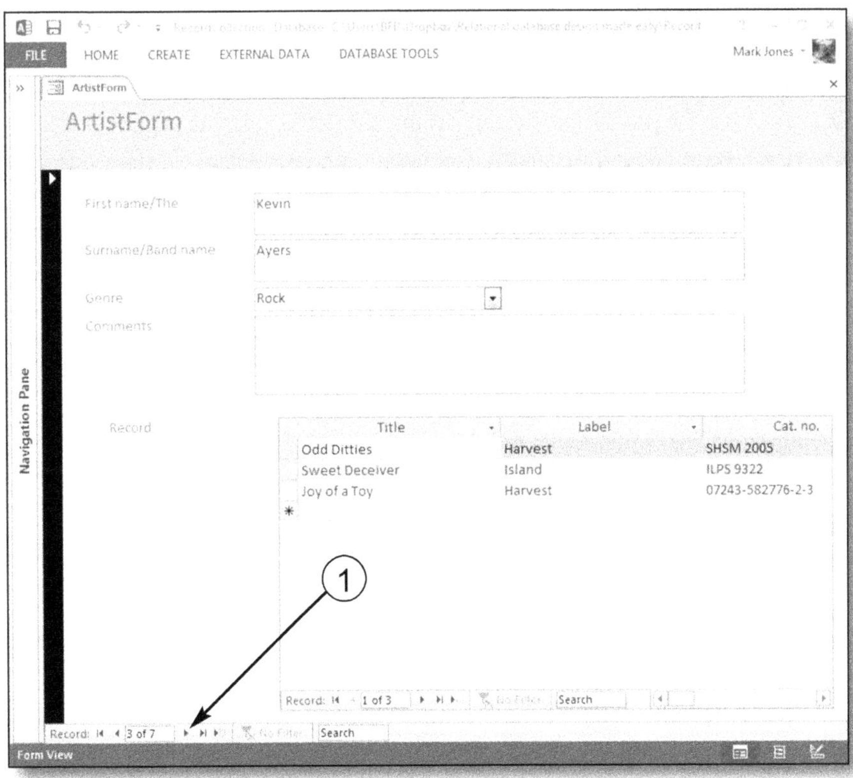

There are a couple of things to note about the form and sub–form. The first is that, because we have already created look–ups in the table, these were created for us automatically when we built the form – they're there in the sub–form as well, but you have to click in the fields before the drop–down appears.

As already mentioned, you can create relationships without creating look–ups, but you would then have to create 'one–off' drop–downs on forms and sub–forms using a wizard. This is fiddly and it is much better not to have to bother.

YOU KEEP MENTIONING WIZARDS; WHAT ARE THEY?

Wizards are (mostly) useful sets of automated steps that give you various choices, as you go through several screens, in order to come out at the other end with something built or done that would otherwise be difficult to do 'by hand'.

Secondly, we can see that there are some obvious formatting problems with various parts of the form and sub–form. For example, some of the fields look rather larger than we really need and we can't see most of the fields in the sub–form.

We can sort these issues out in a second, but bear in mind that we're not going to do too much in the way of fine–tuning how the form looks, such as by adding colours and so on. As previously explained, this book is about getting your database built and working, rather than concentrating on all of the software features available. Besides, I don't have a clue how you might want to make your forms look – everyone is different and I'm not going to try and second–guess what you might want.

One other thing; although as far as we are concerned we have build just one form, Microsoft Access 2013 knows better. If you look at the *Navigation Pane*, you will see that we have two forms listed there. As far as Microsoft Access 2013 is concerned you have just built two forms, one of which lives inside the other.

Sorting out the formatting issues on the form

Before we start, let's just point out that we can't do anything with the sub–form, other than resize it and make the fields the widths that we want, so don't get carried away in design view.

Although design view makes it look as though we can do interesting things to the sub–form, indeed it even lets us go through the motions of doing so, when you then look at the form in the data entry view, nothing will be changed.

To open the form in design view and make it easy to toggle between views:

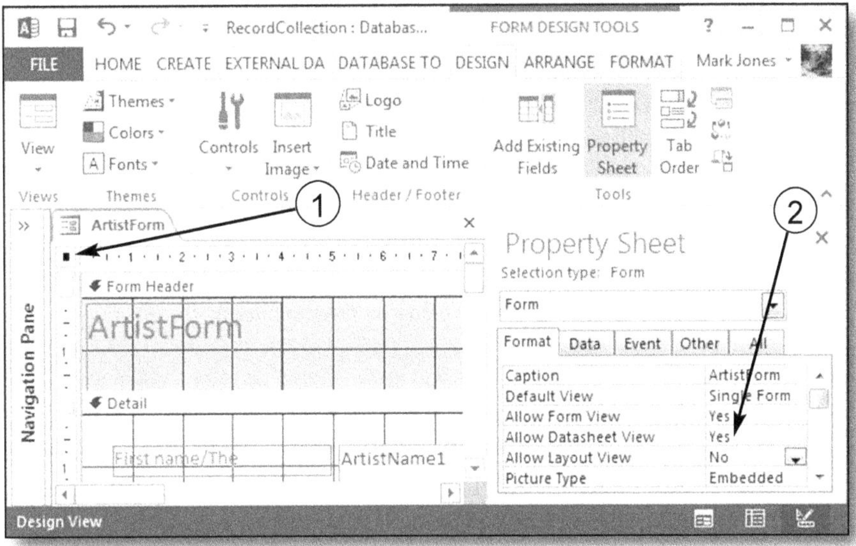

1. In the *Home* tab of the *Ribbon*, click on the downward arrow under the *View* icon and select *Design View.*

2. Make sure that there is a small, black square under the *ArtistForm* tab (1) – if there isn't, i.e. if you've clicked on anything after opening in design view, then click once in the blank square where we want the black box.

3. In the *Ribbon*, click on *Property Sheet* and, in the *Format* tab of the *Property Sheet*, change *Allow Datasheet View* to **Yes** and change *Allow Layout View* to **No** (2).

4. Click again on the *Property Sheet* icon in the *Ribbon* to close the *Property Sheet* down for the moment.

To test what we've just done:

1. Click on the *View* icon in the *Ribbon* (i.e. not on the downward arrow underneath the icon).
2. Notice that, in the normal data entry view of the form, you can now click on the *Design View* icon without having to select it from the drop–down. This means that you can much more easily now toggle between the design and data entry views, which you will be doing rather a lot.
3. Now click on the downward arrow under the icon in the *View* section of the *Ribbon* and notice that you have *Datasheet View* as an option rather than *Layout View*. Datasheet view lets you see the fields in the form in a table–like view, which can be useful if you want to see more than one record at the same time, such as if sorting alphabetically.

I CAN'T FIND THE VIEW ICON IN DESIGN VIEW

Ah, yes, occasionally, depending on what you are doing, Microsoft Access 2013 gets all helpful and moves you to a Ribbon *tab where moving to normal data entry view is not an option. All you need to do is to click on the* Home *tab and you'll see the* View *toggle icon again.*

To resize the sub–form and data entry fields on the main form:

1. Make sure that you are in design view – it can be a bit confusing to start with working out where you are. Basically, if you can see a grid in the background, then you are in design view and if you can't, then you're not.
2. Click on the label that says *Record*, next to the sub–form, then press the *Delete* key on your keyboard.
3. Now click once only on the sub–form – notice that it is now has an orangey–yellow surround with some small, square boxes in each corner and half way along each side. (If you clicked on the sub–form twice, you won't see the surround, in which case, click outside the sub–form *once* and click *once* on the sub–form again.)
4. Click on the square box in the middle of the left–hand edge of the sub–form and drag to the left to make the sub–form wider.
5. Click on the *View* icon to see what your changes look like in the normal data entry view.

6. Go back to design view and do the same with the right–hand side of the sub–form (only dragging to the right, obviously!); notice that it now gives you much more room to work in to the right; don't worry if you can't see all the the data entry fields in the sub–form yet, because we'll sort that out in a minute or so.

7. Toggle back to design view and make changes to the size of the *First name/The* and *Surname/band name* fields (and the sub–form if you want to make further changes to the size) so that they are sensible sizes.

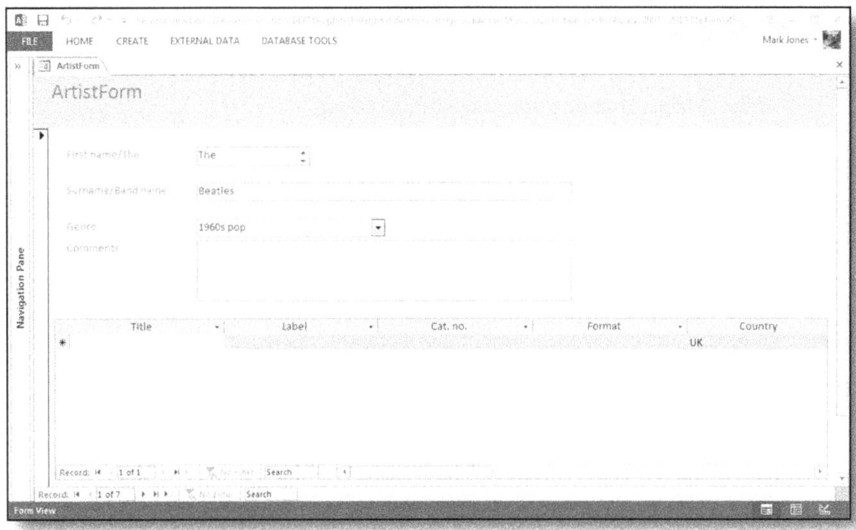

The form may now look similar to the screenshot above. Notice that resizing the top two fields now makes the spacing look a bit wrong. We'll sort that out after rearranging the sub–form fields to make them viewable.

HOW DO YOU HIDE THE RIBBON AND NAVIGATION PANE?

Ah, you've noticed that my screenshots tend to miss out the Ribbon *and the* Navigation Pane. *Although both are useful, they can quite often get in the way when you want a bit of elbow room for doing the design work.*

To hide the Navigation Pane, *click on the double arrow in the top, right–hand corner. To show it again, click anywhere on the thin, vertical* Navigation Pane *bar to the far left of your screen.*

To hide the Ribbon, *hold down the* Ctrl *key on your keyboard and press the* F1 *key. Do the same to re–show the* Ribbon.

To show all the fields in the sub–form:

1. Make sure that you are in data entry view and not in design view.
2. Decrease the width of each column in the sub–form just as you would with a spread sheet; do this by hovering the mouse pointer in–between two headers until a left/right–pointing arrow appears, then hold down the mouse button and drag.
3. If necessary, return to design view to change the size of the sub–form and toggle back to normal data entry view to view your changes.
4. When you are happy with what you see (I always tend to keep the comments fields hidden), hold down the *Ctrl* key on your keyboard and then press the S key to save the changes. Note that this will also save all of the design changes you have made so far.

Before we go ahead and start doing more things to the various objects (known as field controls) on the form, there is some very important information to know about data entry fields and labels.

DATA ENTRY FIELDS AND LABELS

Be very wary of data entry fields – you can resize them and add formatting to your heart's content, but don't be tempted to alter the spelling of the text inside the box (this includes adding spaces). You will know if you have done this accidentally, because in design view you will see a small, green triangle in one corner – or in data entry view the field will say #Name?. *This means that the field has lost contact with the table. The good news is that if you add back the original text, then it reconnects. My advice is be careful!*

Labels, however, are just that – labels. You can change the text in those or even delete them altogether as we did with the label for the Record subform). If you change a label's text and a green triangle appears, then it wasn't the label!

To make the field spacing equal:

1. In design view, click on the *Genre* data entry field (note that the data entry field is the one to the right; the *Genre* rectangle to the left is just the label that tells you what the field is for – see the tip directly above for some very important information).
2. Press the upward arrow key on the keyboard three times to move the field upward; note that the label moves with it even though not highlighted.

3. Click on the *Arrange* tab above the *Ribbon*, then click once on the *ArtistName1* field (not the label, which says *First name/The*).
4. Press and hold down the Shift key on the keyboard and click once on the *ArtistName2* and *Genre* fields respectively (not the labels).
5. In the *Ribbon*, click on the *Size/Space* icon and select *Equal Vertical*; press Ctrl and S on the keyboard to save your changes.
6. Have a look at the other options available from the *Size/Space* and *Align* icon drop–downs and have a play if you like; if you don't like the results, judicious use of the *Undo* icon (1) is recommended (located above the *Home* tab in the *Ribbon*).

The form may now look similar to the screenshot below. Notice that we can now see all of the sub–form fields because of the resizing we've done.

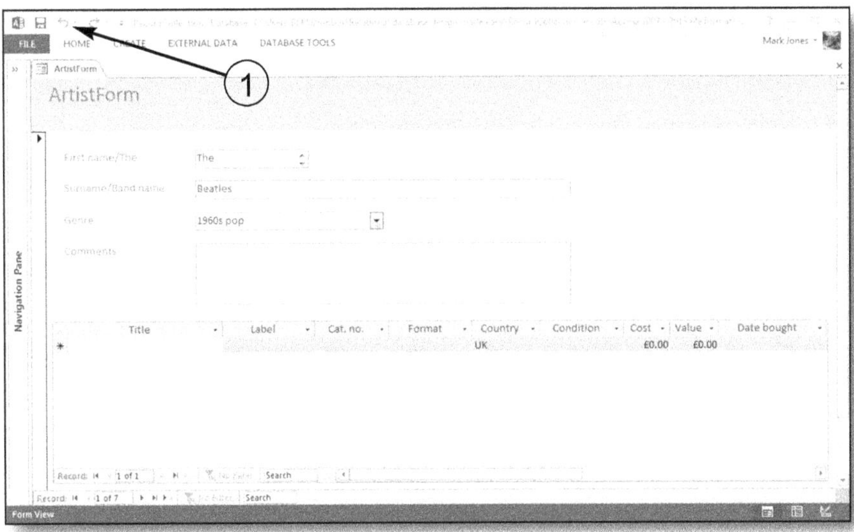

You can do things with colours if you like. Every object on the form, as well as the form itself, can be tailored individually to how you want it to look. In design view, select the *Format* tab from the *Ribbon* and try clicking on various of the objects or backgrounds and trying out some of the options. Don't forget the *Undo* option if you don't like the effect of particular formatting commands.

Additional tasks

We've finished the database from point of view of the building blocks that appertain to the building of *any* database from a paper–based design and are now into the database–specific tasks. These, remember, fall into two categories: those things that your database needs to do for it to be useful to you; those things that will make everyday use of the database easier.

Things that your database needs to do

There wasn't really anything in this particular example, other than being able to calculate the value of the collection, which is inferred by the scenario stating that the database is needed for insurance purposes. Presumably, being able to find out the total value would be useful.

The following introduces a specialised type of query. Most queries you build will probably just be 'filtering' data based on showing records that match one or more pieces of data. This one includes a calculation.

To calculate the total value of the record collection:

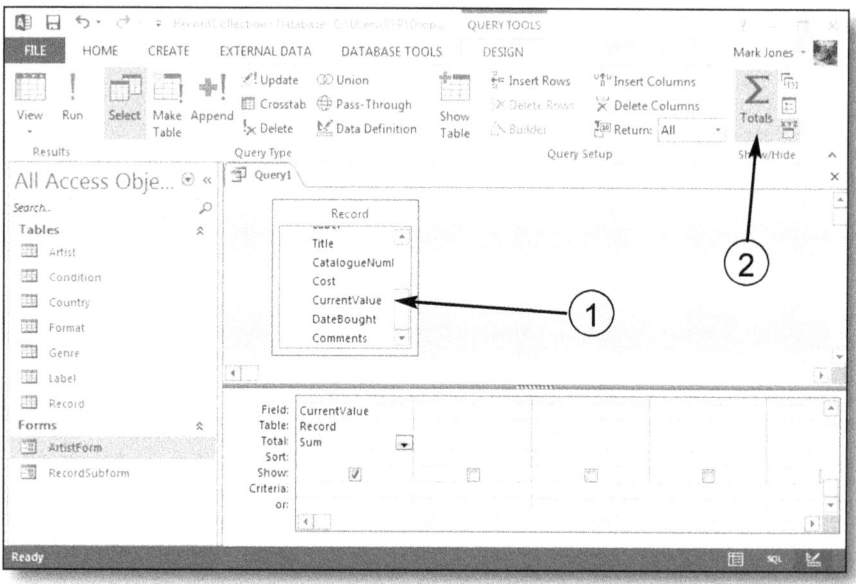

1. Make sure that all tables and forms are closed and click on the *Create* tab above the *Ribbon*.

2. Click on *Query Design* and in the *Show Table* box that opens, double–click on *Record* to add it to the design window, then click on the *Close* button to close the *Show Table* box.
3. In the *Record* table in the design window, scroll down the list of fields and double–click on *CurrentValue* (1) to add it to the grid.
4. In the *Ribbon*, click on the *Totals* icon (2) and note that it adds a new row to the grid that says *Group By*.
5. Click in the field that says *Group By*, click on the drop–down that appears and select *Sum* from the list.
6. Click on the *View* icon in the *Ribbon* to see the query result; there will only be a figure if you have entered in any values for records.
7. Go back to design view (the same way as you do with tables and forms) and click on the *Save* icon above the *File* tab in the *Ribbon*; name the query as **CurrentValue** and save it.

The new query is now saved and so appears in the Navigation Pane. You can run this query at any time by double–clicking on it. Queries are based on the current data in the database, so if you buy more records, the query will show a different value next time you run it.

Why not close the query, open the main form, add a couple of records, including their current value, close the form then run the query again?

Things to make using your database easier to use

There are two things that make all the difference to everyday use, both of which are small things in themselves, but ones which tend to provide that 'niggle' factor:

> **1.** Getting Microsoft Access 2013 to open directly into the main data entry form without having to open it 'manually' from the *Navigation Pane* once the database is opened.
> **2.** Making navigation between records easier.

The first requires building a *macro* (i.e. one or more commands rolled up into one item) and giving it a specific name. As for the second, the navigation buttons at the bottom of the data entry screen are small and fiddly to click (and see, now that I've got to a certain age) and I've never yet discovered any keyboard commands that can be used to 'press' these buttons (which doesn't mean that there aren't any, just that I've never managed to discover them in the last twenty years, despite occasional half–hearted searching).

Creating buttons for navigation has two advantages, which are that you can tab to the buttons and 'click' them by pressing *Enter* on the keyboard (as well as using the mouse, of course); also, you can assign keyboard shortcuts to them so that you don't have to tab all the way to a button to use it.

To get Microsoft Access 2013 to open directly into the main data entry form:

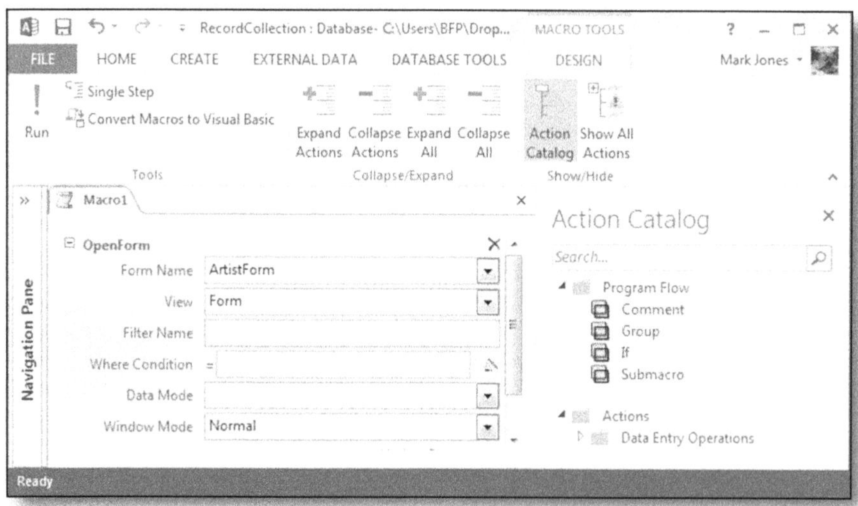

1. Make sure that all objects are closed, click on the *Create* tab above the *Ribbon* and then click on *Macro* in the *Ribbon*.
2. Click on the drop–down in the only available field and select *OpenForm*.
3. Choose *ArtistForm* from the *Form Name* drop–down and click the *Save* icon above the *File* tab.
4. Name the macro as **Autoexec** (exactly as spelled here, though all in lower case is fine) and save it, then close Microsoft Access 2013.
5. Reopen *RecordCollection.accdb* – if it doesn't open the form directly on the database opening, then go back and see what you did wrong (usually a misspelling of 'autoexec').

You could, whilst creating the macro, get the form to open a specific record, or an empty record, this last of which is useful if the main purpose of your form is to add new records rather, than in this case, to add sub–form records to (mostly) pre–exisiting artists.

We'll now move to the second task, adding navigation buttons. Once we've worked through one example you can add the rest on your own.

To add a navigation button complete with keyboard control command to the form:

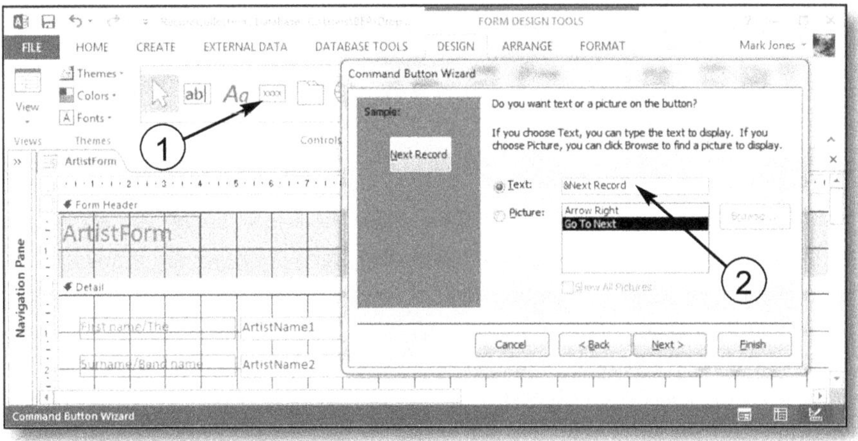

1. Make sure all objects are closed, then open *ArtistForm* in design view.
2. In the *Controls* section of the *Ribbon*, click on the *Button* control (1) and then click on the form approximately where you want the button to appear.

3. In the *Command Button Wizard* that opens, select the *Go To Next Record* action from the default *Record Navigation* category and then click on *Next*.
4. Click in the *Text* field that says *Next Record*, type **&** in front of the *N* (2) and click on *Next*.
5. Name the button **ButtonNextRecord** and click on *Finish*.
6. Toggle to data entry view and click on your new button to go to the next record; now hold down the *Alt* key on the keyboard and press *N* to go to the next record again.

You can now create the following buttons, all from the *Record Navigation* category in the wizard, on your own:

- *Go To First Record*
- *Go To Last Record*
- *Go To Previous Record*
- *Find Record*

Don't forget to put an **&** in front of whichever letter you want to form part of the keyboard command, such as **&Previous Record** for the keyboard command to be *Alt* + *P*. Just in case you were going to ask, you can't use the same letter twice on the same form.

Also give each button a sensible name, such as **ButtonPreviousRecord**, so that you know which button is which when we come, in a minute, to sorting out in which order we want to tab through the buttons.

Once you've created the buttons, you can move them to wherever you want them to be, either by clicking once on the button and using the keyboard arrow keys or by clicking once, holding the mouse button down and dragging it to a new position.

All we need to do now is to make sure that the tab order (i.e. the movement from field to field and to added objects, such as sub–forms and buttons) is exactly how we want it. Whilst we're at it, note that letting the database tab you into a sub–form, which is the default setting, can have some issues because, you then have to tab through every data entry field of every record in that sub–form before you tab out the other end to move on to the next main form record.

To ensure that the buttons are in the correct order for tabbing:

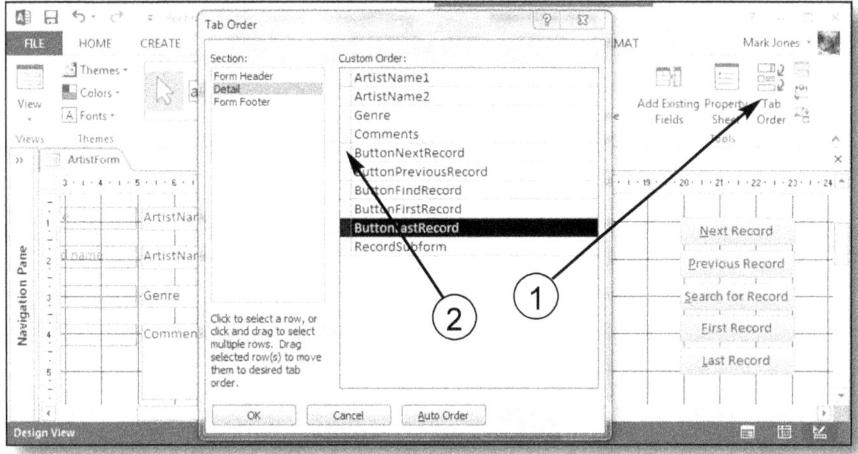

1. In design view, click on the *Tab Order* icon (1) in the *Ribbon*.
2. Click on the small, grey rectangle (2) to the immediate left of *ButtonNextRecord* to highlight the whole row, then click again on the rectangle and drag it above the *RecordSubform* row; now you can see why we name the buttons in such a way that we know what each does.
3. Do the same with the other buttons, moving them where you want them.
4. Click *OK*, then go to normal data entry view and test the tab changes.

To stop tabbing into the sub–form:

1. In design view click once only on the sub–form and click on *Property Sheet* in the *Ribbon*.
2. Click on the *Other* tab in *Property Sheet* and set *Tab Stop* to *No*.
3. Save the form, then go to data entry view and test the tab changes.

If you don't want to tab to the navigation buttons, then you could remove them from the tabbing list in exactly the same way as above.

We could do other things, but when it comes down to it, the options you have for fine–tuning are almost limitless. My advice is to get any data entry forms that you will be using often into a state where you find them easy to use. You can play with colours and so on or add images but, when all is said and done, the database is there to do a job. Once it lets you do that job comfortably, then it is finished as far as development work goes.

FURTHER EXAMPLES

Just as a quick reminder, before we get started on our own, of the four building blocks for building relational databases:

1. Build your tables.
2. Add the relationships.
3. Test your database.
4. Set up the data entry form(s).

For the further examples, we're presented with just the relational design and the details of each table that you need to build, complete with field names, data types, format/size and a list of suggested captions.

Only at those points where there is something that we've not yet come across is there a list of detailed steps of what to do. Effectively, this is only where you want to choose a name from a drop–down and in the additional tasks where certain things have been stipulated as being necessary.

The above, as you work through these two further examples, will confirm to you that, as far as the building blocks are concerned, the building of one database is pretty much the same as any other database. You build the tables the same way; you assign the keys in the same way; you add look–ups/relationships in the same way. The only difference is in the actual paper design, which tells you how you need to join the various tables together. The same goes for testing any database: you put the test data into the tables that feed drop–downs first, then you test the main tables by adding data manually and/or from drop–downs; you test any sub–tables in the same way. Forms with sub–forms too are all built in exactly the same way. And if your design doesn't need a sub–form, then it's easier still.

Small business scenario

The scenario is as follows:

> *I want to be able to keep track of expenditure for each project I undertake – that is, I want to know what I spend, the date, which company or person I'm paying, how much I'm spending on each transaction and how I pay – i.e. debit card, credit card, credit, cash etc. I need to be able to distinguish between services and actual items, which is something that I keep forgetting to keep track of. A prompt in the database will be very useful on this score. By the way, the items bought are hardly ever the same from project to project.*
>
> *I also need to know which customer the project relates to so that I know who to bill for expenses to date. Customers pay for ongoing expenses during the life of the project and then pay the remainder of the originally agreed sum on project completion. Most customers are repeat customers.*
>
> *It would be really nice if the database could print out the interim invoices for me to send too, or is that too much to ask? At the very least I need to know which items have already been invoiced for.*

The parts that relate to additional tasks rather than to the building blocks are:

1. The prompt. This requires building a pop–up message whenever someone forgets to enter that particular piece of data. Because of this we will have to make the field a short text field, instead of, as we normally would with only two choices on offer, a tick box. This is explained later.
2. The printing out of invoices. This has to do with output, not input – though required outputs are good for hinting at some of the bits that you may have forgotten to otherwise write about.

BUILDING YOUR TABLES: CHECKLIST

For each table:

__1.__ Create data entry fields.

__2.__ Assign data type and specify size and/or format.

__3.__ Create captions where required.

__4.__ Add any required properties, such as default value.

__5.__ Assign primary key; ensure that foreign keys are present and set correctly.

__6.__ Save and name the table.

Field name (key)	Data type	Size/format	Caption
CustomerKey (PK)	Auto Number	—	Customer code
CustomerName1	Short Text	50	First name
CustomerName2	Short Text	50	Last name/Organisation
Address1	Short Text	100	Address line 1
Address2	Short Text	100	Address line 2
Address3	Short Text	100	Address line 3
Town	Short Text	100	—
Postcode	Short Text	20	—
Telephone	Short Text	100	—
Email	Short Text	200	—
Comments	Long Text	—	—

Table 9. The *Customer* table.

Field name (key)	Data type	Size/format	Caption
InvoiceNumber (PK)	Short Text	20	Invoice no.
DateSent	Date/Time	Long Date	Date sent
DatePaid	Date/Time	Long Date	Date paid
Comments	Long Text	—	—

Table 10. The *InvoiceNumber* table.

Field name (key)	Data type	Size/format	Caption
ItemKey (PK)	Auto Number	—	Item code
InvoiceNumber (FK)	Short Text	20	Invoice no.
PaymentMethod (FK)	Short Text	30	Payment method
ProjectKey (FK)	Number	Long Integer	Project
SupplierKey (FK)	Number	Long Integer	Supplier
Item	Short Text	100	—
Service	Short Text	10	Service or item?
Cost	Currency	£	—
DateBought	Date/Time	Long Date	Date bought
Comments	Long Text	Long Text	—

Table 11. The *Item* table.

Field name (key)	Data type	Size/format	Caption
PaymentMethod (PK)	Short Text	30	Payment method
Comments	Long Text	—	—

Table 12. The *PaymentMethod* table.

Field name (key)	Data type	Size/format	Caption
ProjectKey (PK)	Auto Number	—	Project code
CustomerKey (FK)	Number	Long Integer	Customer
ProjectName	Short Text	100	Project name
AgreedCost	Currency	£	Agreed cost
Comments	Long Text	—	—

Table 13. The *Project* table.

Field name (key)	Data type	Size/format	Caption
SupplierKey (PK)	Auto Number	—	Supplier code
SupplierName1	Short Text	50	First name
SupplierName2	Short Text	50	Surname/Organisation
Address1	Short Text	100	Address line 1
Address2	Short Text	100	Address line 2
Address3	Short Text	100	Address line 3
Town	Short Text	100	—
Postcode	Short Text	20	—
Telephone	Short Text	100	—
Email	Short Text	200	—
Comments	Long Text	—	—

Table 14. The *Supplier* table.

Don't forget that you don't include either *(PK)* or *(FK)* in the names you give to those particular fields. These are included to remind you to double–check that you have assigned the primary key and have given all primary and foreign keys the correct data types and field size/format.

With other fields you can always go back to the design view of the table and update them later if you got it wrong (which you'll generally know the moment you try to type data into them), but with primary and foreign keys the best way forward is to get them right first go. Otherwise, troubleshooting when Microsoft Access 2013 prevents you from creating look–ups/relationships can be fraught with difficulties if you don't know what you're doing.

ADDING THE RELATIONSHIPS: CHECKLIST

1. For all relationships, create look–ups, which will automatically create drop–downs on any forms you subsequently build.

2. Where the drop–down needs to contain a person's name or alternative text to a code, set the drop–down to display the required data.

3. Finish all relationships in the Relationships window.

4. Save the relationships.

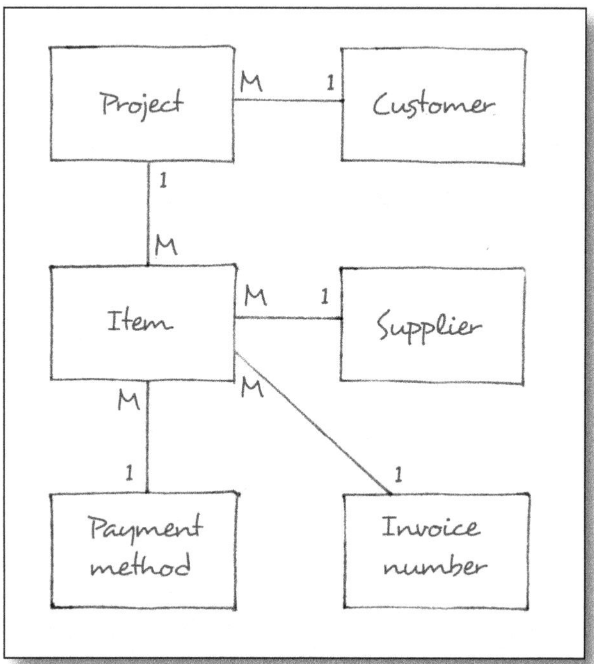

Figure 2. The small business project design showing the relationships that you will need to set.

Create the following relationships in the same way as previously, i.e. by creating look–ups and then finishing the relationships off in the *Relationships* window (remember when going through the *Lookup Wizard* from from within the *Item* table to select only the primary key from the relevant related tables, otherwise we'll see the wrong data in the drop–downs):

- *Item* and *PaymentMethod*
- *Item* and *InvoiceNumber*

Note that you may need to prompt the *Relationships* window to show you one or more tables by using the *Show Table* icon in the *Ribbon*.

Don't yet set up the look–ups/relationships between *Item* and *Project*, *Project* and *Customer* or *Item* and *Supplier* because we need to do these a slightly different way to those that you've already seen. We'll work though setting the first two of these look–up/relationships and then you can do the look–up/relationship between *Item* and *Supplier* yourself, because this done exactly the same way as between *Project* and *Customer*.

The look–up between *Item* and *Project* is different to the others that we have seen because we will, depending on the data entry forms we create later, want to see the project name in the drop–down instead of the project code – just seeing the code, which is a number set by an auto number field, doesn't tell us much, but the project name does.

As for the other two lookups/relationships, we want to see the contents of two fields in the drop–down instead of just the code field, so we have to do something slightly different than with the *Item* to *Project* look–up/relationship.

To set up the look–up/relationship between *Item* and *Project*:

1. Open the *Item* table in design view, click on the *Data Type* field for *ProjectKey*, choose *Lookup Wizard...* from the drop–down and click *Next*.
2. Select *Table: Project*, click on *Next*, then double–click first on *ProjectKey* and then on *ProjectName* to move them to the *Selected Fields* box – it is important that you do this in the order stated.
3. Click *Next* and select to sort by *ProjectName*, then click on *Next* and *Next* again – again, it important that you choose the correct field in this step, otherwise the drop–down will not be sorted in alphabetical order.
4. Tick *Enable Data Integrity*, click *Finish* and choose to save the table; then close the table.
5. Click on the *Database Tools* tab above the *Ribbon*, open the *Relationships* window, complete the relationship between the two tables in the usual way, then close the *Relationships* window and save changes.

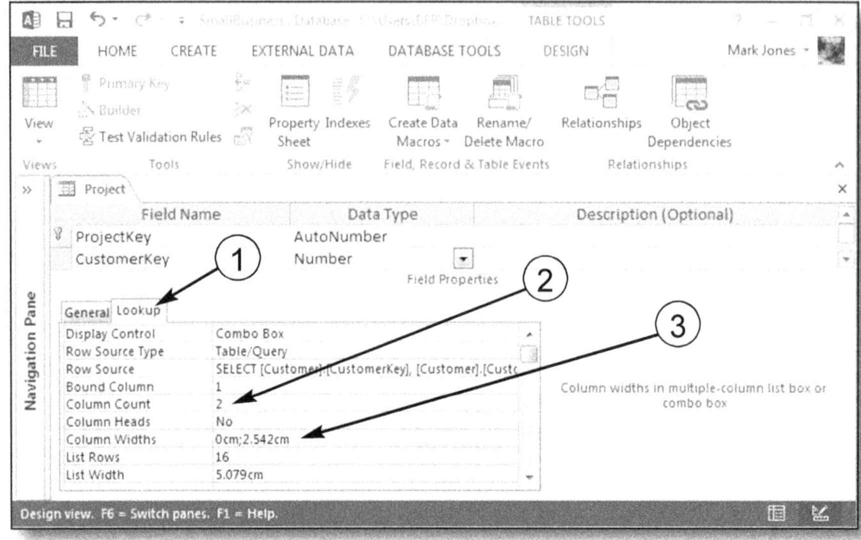

To set up the look–up/relationship between *Project* and *Customer*:

1. Open the *Project* table in design view, click on the *Data Type* field for *CustomerKey*, select *Lookup Wizard...* from the drop–down and click *Next*.
2. Select *Table: Customer*, click on *Next*, then double–click first on *CustomerKey* and then on *CustomerName1* and *CustomerName2* to move them to the *Selected Fields* box.
3. Click *Next* and select to sort by *CustomerName2*, then click on *Next* and *Next* again.
4. Tick *Enable Data Integrity*, click *Finish* and choose to save the table.
5. Click on the *Lookup* tab (1) in the *Field Properties* at the bottom of the design view window and in *Row Source* remove the comma from the end of *[Customer].[CustomerName1],* and replace with **& " " &** (as in a space, ampersand, space, double speech marks, space, double speechmarks, space, ampersand and a final space); the whole should now read:

SELECT [Customer].[CustomerKey], [Customer].[CustomerName1] & " " & [Customer].[CustomerName2] FROM Customer ORDER BY [CustomerName2];

6. Change *Column Count* (2) to 2 and change the contents of *Column Widths* (3) from *0cm;2.54cm;2.54cm* to **0cm;2.54cm** (i.e. remove the third figure). The final two figures may be different to the above example; this doesn't matter, just remove the final figure, whatever it is. The second figure may change automatically when you do this; again, don't worry!

7. Save and close the table, then click on the *Database Tools* tab above the *Ribbon*, open the *Relationships* window and complete the relationship between the two tables in the usual way; close the *Relationships* window and save when prompted.

Now create the look–up/relationship between the *Item* and *Supplier* tables, though bearing in mind that the text in *Row Source* in the *Lookup* tab will be as follows:

SELECT [Supplier].[SupplierKey], [Supplier].[SupplierName1] & " " & [Supplier].[SupplierName2] FROM Supplier ORDER BY [SupplierName2];

Your Relationships window should now, with a bit of rearranging and tidying up, look like the following screenshot:

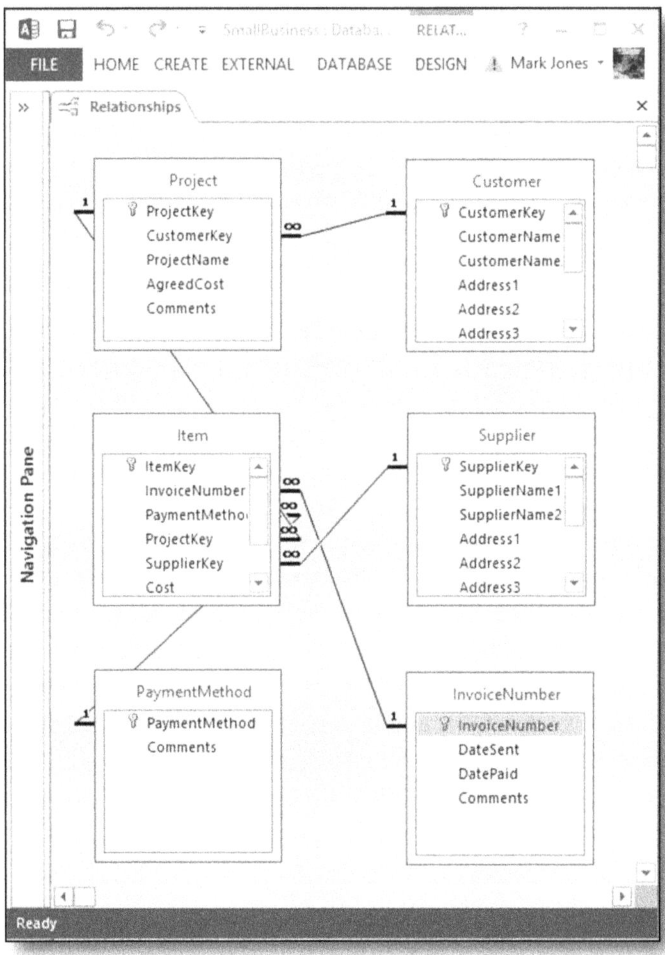

Now we need to enter some test data.

TEST YOUR DATABASE: CHECKLIST

1. Enter test data into each look–up table.

2. Enter one or two records into your main table, choosing data from all drop–downs.

3. Check the data in sub–tables.

4. If you have a sub–table where you expected a drop–down, or vice versa, then go back and see where you went wrong.

Just make up some data for testing the database. For the look–up tables enter about three records apiece so that you have a few options for each drop–down in the *Project* and *Item* tables.

Just one thing, don't type anything into the *Service* field in the *Item* table yet because we need to do some work on this field in a few seconds so that it automatically flags up if someone forgets to enter data into it, as per the request in the original scenario. This needs to be done before we create the data entry form because we need to set up a stand alone look–up (i.e. not based on a table) which we want later to automatically create a drop–down when we create the form.

To create a stand alone look–up for the *Service* field:

1. Open the *Item* table in design view, click on the *Data Type* field for *Service* and choose *Lookup Wizard...* from the drop–down.
2. This time, select *I will type in the values that I want* and click on *Next*.
3. Under *Col1* type **Item** into the top field and **Service** into the field directly below, then click on *Next* and tick the *Limit to List* box.
4. Click on *Finish* and save the table.

We would usually have made this a tick box because, when there are only two options, a tick box is usually the best solution. However, setting this to flag if left empty would be, not impossible, but difficult – because one option for a tick box is not to be ticked! This, then, shows that the design plan can (and usually does) change during development – this field was highlighted in the sister book, *Database Design Made Easy*, as a *Yes/No* field, but this is the real world and plans change based on how Microsoft Access 2013 lets you do the things that you need to do.

To create a pop–up message if nothing is entered into the field:

1. In the *Field Properties* for *Service*, click on *Required* and choose *Yes* from the drop–down.
2. Save and close the table, saying *OK* to the warning message that pops–up warning tha you have changed data integrity rules.
3. Add a new record to the *Item* table, deliberately missing out the *Service* field (though notice that this field now has a drop–down); try to save this record or move on to a new record and view the pop–up message.

Now that we've done this, we can build the data entry form with sub–form, which will pick up both the drop–down we've just created by building the look–up above as well as the pop–up message.

SET UP YOUR DATA ENTRY FORMS: CHECKLIST

1. Create data entry form(s) using the Form Wizard *option so as to create any required sub–forms automatically.*
2. If you need more than one sub–form on a form, create and add these individually.
3. Fine–tune the data entry form to look and work how you want.
4. Save each form as you make changes to it.

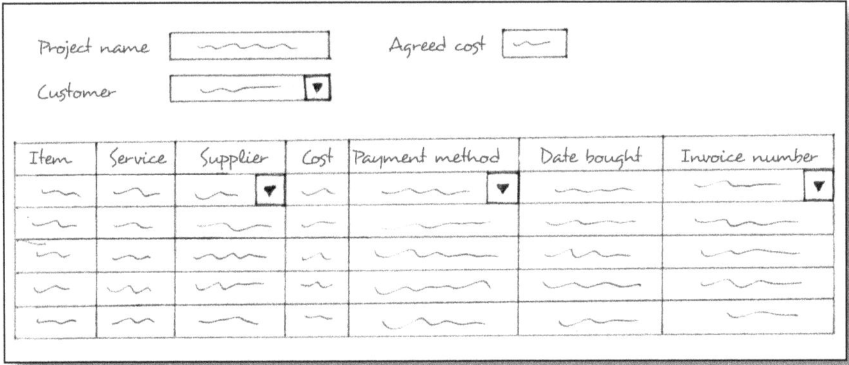

This is fairly straightforward, if a bit fiddly when it comes to any fine–tuning that you might want to do. So all I'll do here is to remind you that the main form puts data into the *Project* table and the sub–form puts data into the Item table, so these are the tables you want to choose the above fields from (not forgetting to also add the two *Comments* fields, which were excluded from the original hand–drawn design) when working through the *Form Wizard*.

Also, remember that when it comes to adding the sub–form fields you don't need to add either *ProjectKey* or *ItemKey* to the *Selected Fields* box. On the one hand Microsoft Access 2013 can already work out the relationship between the two tables, so doesn't need *ProjectKey*, and *ItemKey* is just an auto number so there is no point in seeing it in the sub–form. The same goes for ProjectKey – it is just an auto number, so there is no real benefit to including it in the main form.

Also, don't forget that the convention used in listing the fields for each table shows all the foreign keys directly below the primary key. This will not be the order in which you want to add the fields to the *Selected Fields* box whilst working through the wizard. Have a look at the hand–drawn form design to see the field order – though there's nothing to stop you adding these in any order that you want.

Your main form and sub–form should look something like the screenshot below:

As far as the building blocks go, we have completed the database now. Tables, relationships and main data entry form are all finished and we have added test data to make sure that our relational design works.

There are a few additional tasks, however, that need to be done to ensure that the database will be useful in context. Firstly, we could add a button to view customer contact details. Secondly, we need some way of showing which items have already been invoiced and to print out invoices for items/services not yet invoiced. Lastly, we also need an easy way of setting up a new invoice – a button will do for this.

To view customer details we need to create a data entry form based on the *Customer* table and then we can create a button to open just the record we want to see. The invoicing requires a little more in the way of piggery jokery.

To create a button that opens the correct customer record:

1. Create a form based on the *Customer* table using the *Form Wizard* (do the same as we have previously, but only using the one table; move all fields from the table over to the *Selected Fields* box).
2. Close the new *Customer* form (or whatever you decided to call it) and open the *Project* form in design view.
3. Start the *Button Wizard* as you did previously, only click on *Form Operations* in the *Categories* box, then select *Open Form* from the *Actions* box and click on *Next*.
4. In the next window select *Customer*, click on *Next*, select *Open the form and find specific data to display* and click on *Next*.
5. In the *Project* box select *CustomerKey* by clicking once only, then select *CustomerKey* in the *Customer* box, click on the <-> box and click on *Next*.
6. In the *Text* box change the current text to **View customer details** and click on *Next*.
7. Call the button **ButtonOpenCustomerForm**, add an **&** in front of whichever letter you want to use for the keyboard shortcut, and then click on *Finish*.
8. Move the button to where you want it and modify the tabbing order if necessary (or remove the button from tabbing if you want); then view the form in normal data entry view and try out the button from one or more records. Don't forget to save changes.

You will probably want to redesign the *Customer* form, which I'll leave you to do. One thing, however, as that you will probably want the *Customer* form to open as a 'pop–up' so that you can still see the *Project* form underneath.

To make the *Customer* form open in a pop–up window:

1. Open the *Customer* form in design view and open the *Property Sheet*. Do not click anywhere else in the meantime, or you will not be looking at the overall form properties (the small, black box should show in the top, left–hand corner of the form, remember).
2. In the *Data* tab, click in *Pop Up* and select *Yes* from the drop–down.
3. Close the form, save changes and test out the button on the *Project* form again.

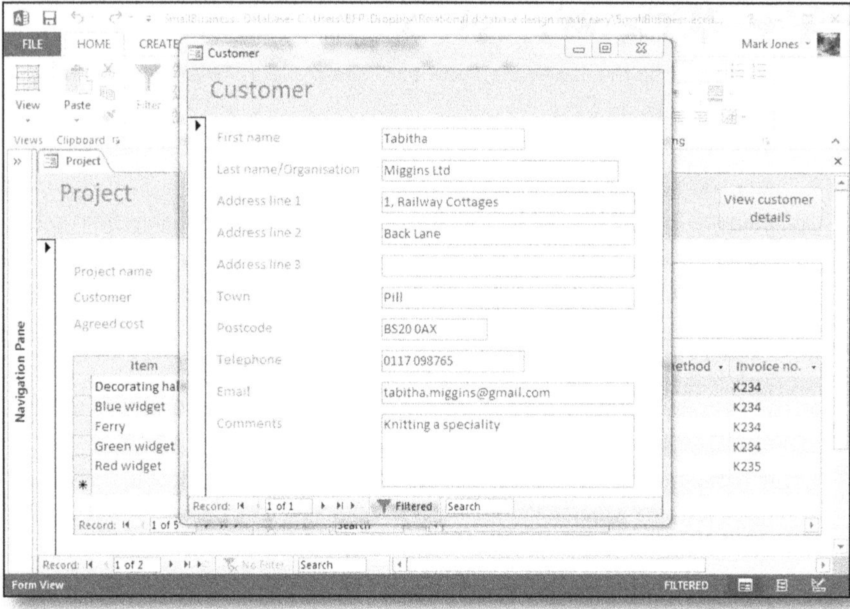

Have you noticed that I'm showing you less screenshots by the way? You should be starting to get a feel for finding your way around Microsoft Access 2013 by now. If you still don't know what you are doing or why, or where anything is, then it might be a good idea to go back and read/work through the worked example again before you make a start on your own database.

To have your database create an invoice for uninvoiced items requires a few steps. As above, there are lots of different ways that this can be done, some of which are more difficult than others and require expert skills. We're going to do it a 'cheap and cheerful' way. My take on database development has always been that if it does the job and does it easily, then a small amount of 'clunkiness' is more than acceptable. You may disagree!

First we need to build a query to show unpaid invoices (this will show both those invoiced but as yet unpaid and those not yet invoiced, for reasons that will become clear later); then we need to build a report based on the query; then we could build a button to open the invoice report – or just open it from the *Navigation Pane*.

To build the query:

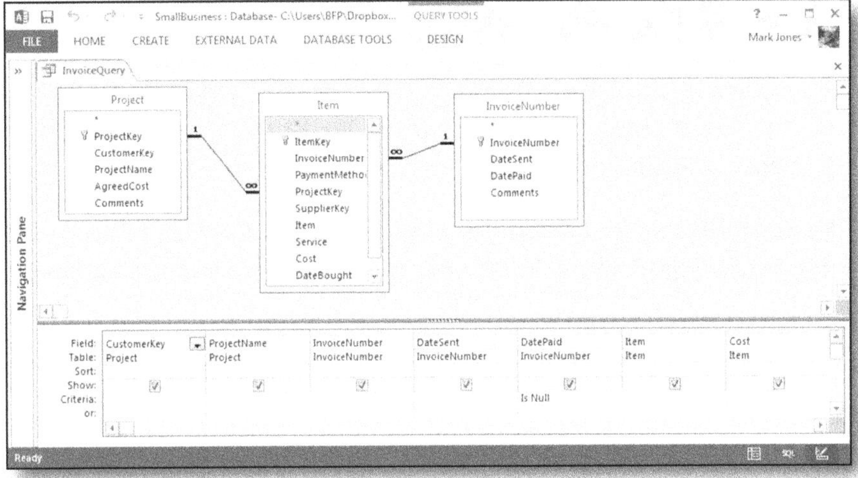

1. Make sure that all objects are closed, click on the *Create* tab and select *Query Design*.
2. From the *Show Table* pop–up select the *Project*, *Item* and *InvoiceNumber* tables (we don't need the *Customer* table because we already have the customer details in the *Project* table).
3. From the *Project* table add *CustomerKey* and *ProjectName* to the grid; from the *InvoiceNumber* table add *InvoiceNumber*, *DateSent* and *DatePaid*; from the *Item* table add *Item* and *Cost*.
4. In *DatePaid* type **Is Null** in the *Criteria* row – note: Microsoft Access 2013 might add *IsNull(* for you automatically; if it does, then delete the open bracket and add a space between the two words – then save and close the query, calling it *InvoiceQuery*.

To build the report:

> **1.** In the *Create* tab click on *Report Wizard* and select *Query: InvoiceQuery* from the *Tables/Queries* drop–down.
> **2.** Add all the fields except for *DatePaid* to the *Selected Field* box (we need *DatePaid* in the query to filter the data we want to see but we don't need it on the report), click *Next*, make sure that *by Project* is selected and click *Next* again.
> **3.** Double–click on *InvoiceNumber* to add it to a separate box, then click *Next* and *Next* again.
> **4.** Choose *Outline*, followed by *Next*, then name the report as **Invoice** and click on *Finish*.

This has created a report showing all projects for which there are as yet unpaid items, including those where the customer has already been invoiced, but has not yet paid. The reason for this is that the report can be filtered to show (and print) invoices for individual invoice numbers. This means that we can use the same report to print follow–up invoices where an invoice remains unpaid as well as for invoice numbers that have not previously been invoiced for.

The only problem is that the report doesn't look too good. Usually, at least one field will appear in boxes, whilst others do not. Also, the alternate line shading, whilst looking good on basic reports, does not look good in grouped reports (this one is grouped by customer/project name and invoice number). We could also do with creating a calculation to add up all of the items on each so that the customer knows what they are expected to pay. We could have done this in the wizard, but it tends to add some confusing text, so we'll do it 'by hand' instead.

Note that when modifying a report, you need to click on the *View* drop–down and select *Print Preview* each time to view any modifications. Reports are quite confusing in design view, so it's good to check often to see if you are modifying the bit that you think you are modifying. The *Undo* icon tends to be very useful.

To modify the report:

1. Click on *Close Print Preview*, which opens up design view, and click on any field that has a boxed outline; in *Property Sheet*, select the *Format* tab and change *Border Style* to *Transparent*.
2. Click on the background in the *CustomerKey Header* secton and in the *Property Sheet*, again in the *Format* tab, change *Alternate Back Color* to *No Color*, do the same for the *InvoiceNumber Header* and *Detail* sections.
3. Click again on the background in *InvoiceNumber Header*, and in *Propery Sheet* (*Format* tab, yet again) click in the *Back Color* option, then click on the button with three dots that appears and select a light grey from the various colour options. You will need to do this again for the field in this section of the report (but not for the label) otherwise it will remain the original colour.
4. In *InvoiceNumber Header*, delete the three labels (the ones with the small green triangle in the top, left–hand corner) and drag the top of the *Detail* bar upwards to make the section shorter.
5. In the *Detail* section, move the fields and resize them if necessary, so that they look neat and tidy. Do this in the other sections if you want.
6. In the *Ribbon*, click on the *Group and Sort* icon to open the *Group, Sort, and Totals* window at the bottom of the screen. Now click on *Group on InvoiceNumber* and click *More*. Click on the downward arrow next to *Without a footer section* and select *With a footer section*. Click on the icon in the *Ribbon* again to close the window.
7. In the *Ribbon*, click on *Text Box* in the *Controls* section (it's the icon with *ab|* next to the mouse pointer icon) and click once in the newly created *InvoiceNumber Footer* section. In the text box that now appears change *Unbound* to **=Sum(Cost)** and change the label from *Text15* (or similar) to **Total cost**. Move and/or resize the field and label if you want.
8. Click on the new field – the one that says *=Sum(Cost)* – and in the *Format* tab in the *Property Sheet*, click in *Format* and from the drop–down choose *Currency*. You might as well keep the box around this field because it quite nicely highlights the full invoice amount.

It is possible to lose days fine–tuning reports. To my mind they tend to be even more fiddly that forms in this respect. It should come as no surprise that my advice is to get the report looking respectable and then leave it be. Once it does what it needs to do and looks decent enough, then that is the time to stop fiddling with it.

To view, filter and print the data shown in the report:

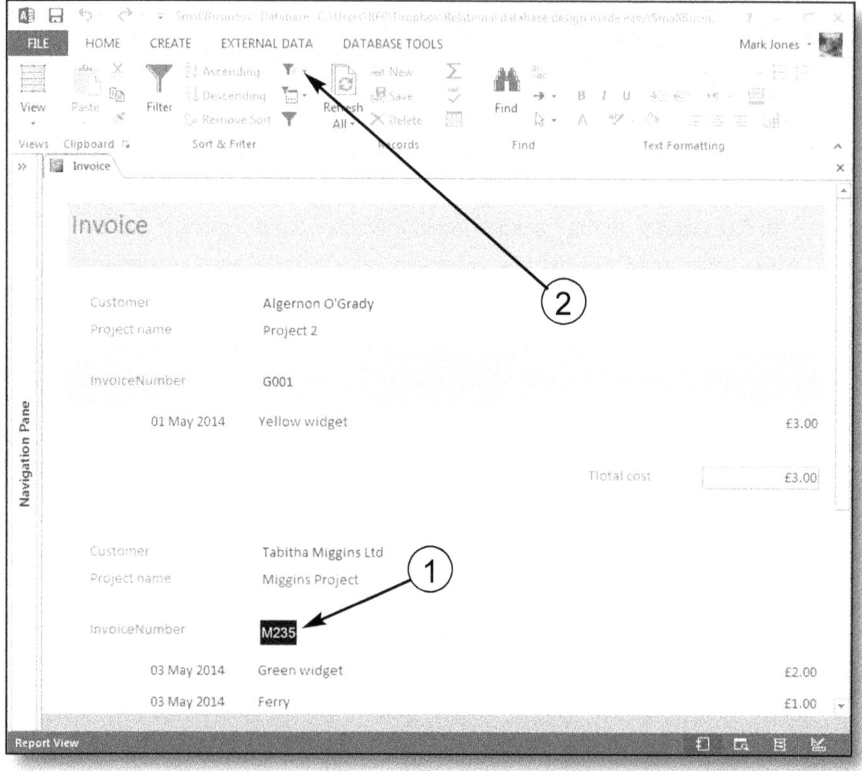

1. Click on the downward arrow under the *View* icon in the *Ribbon* and choose *Report View*.

2. Double–click on one of the invoice numbers to highlight it (1) and, in the *Ribbon*, click on *Selection* in the *Sort & Filter* section (2), then select *Equals* (whatever invoice number you highlighted will appear in speech marks after *Equals*, for example, *Equals "M235"*).

3. Click on the downward arrow under the *View* icon in the *Ribbon* and choose *Print Preview*. Only the filtered data will show and you can print out or save the invoice as a pdf (to save the invoice as a pdf, right–click on the filtered report in *Print Preview* and select *Export* from the menu that pops up).

4. To remove the filter from the report, click on *Close Print Preview*, which takes you back to *Report View*, then click on *Toggle Filter* in the *Ribbon*.

To add a button to the *Project* form to open the invoice report is fairly straightforward, so we won't work through it here. Suffice to say that if you can create a button to open a form, as we already have done for the *Customer* form, then you will have no problems creating a button to open the *Invoice* report. Just choose *Report Operations* from the *Categories* box and you're almost there.

However, setting up a button to set up a new invoice number is a bit convoluted (you can't choose an invoice number in the item sub–form until you've created a record for that invoice number, remember). The problem here is is that you can't use the *Button Wizard* to open a table. What you have to do is create a macro that opens the table and then assign that macro to a button.

To create the macro to open the *InvoiceNumber* table:

1. Close any open objects and in the *Create* tab, select *Macro*.
2. From the drop–down in the only visible field choose *OpenTable* and select *InvoiceNumber* from the *Table Name* drop–down.
3. Close the macro and name it as **OpenInvoiceNumberTableMacro**.

Note that you could set the macro to open a blank, new record by changing *Data Mode* to *Add*, but I tend to find it more useful to see existing records, so as to remind myself of any invoice number naming conventions. It's up to you – you can always modify the macro later by right–clicking on it in the *Navigation Pane* and opening it in design view, just like you do to modify all the other objects.

To create the button:

1. Open the *Project* form in design view and start the *Button Wizard*.
2. In *Categories*, select *Miscellaneous* and in *Actions* select *Run Macro*, then click *Next* and *Next* again (you only have one macro, so you don't need to choose it from a list).
3. Change the *Text* option to **Add new invoice number** and click on *Next*.
4. Name the button as **ButtonOpenInvoiceNumberTable**, click on *Finish* and move and size the button as required (don't forget to change tabbing order or remove from tabbing if required).

That looks to me like a finished database (short of adding navigation buttons and setting an autoexec macro, which I can leave you to do). As mentioned, you can fiddle with the forms and reports to your heart's content, but once it does what it needs to do, then it's finished.

Research scenario

There are no prizes for guessing that you will be getting very little help with this example. Multiple forms are required – but that shouldn't be an issue because you created two forms in the last example. The only real difference is the requirement for multiple sub–forms in the same form. You can only add one sub–form using the *Form Wizard*, so I'll show how to add the other two sub–forms in a 'sneaky' way.

The scenario is as follows:

> *I'm researching into specific aspects of inflammatory bowel disease (IBD). There are eight possible types of IBD for the purposes of this research and each of the 100 patients that have agreed to partake in the project has already been diagnosed with one of these eight types. I need to know which type of IBD any given person has.*
>
> *The main thrust of the research requires me to keep track of all routine (i.e. pre–arranged) or emergency visits made to the hospital by each patient. For each visit I need to record the date and time, which doctor the patient saw, if there were any symptoms recorded and what, if any, treatment was prescribed. I also need to record the discharge date if any patients were kept in hospital. That also means I have to be able to record the date of each individual consultation, treatment and so on, if not the same day as admission/appointment.*
>
> *The main problem is that it is possible that the patient may be seen by more than one doctor in any given visit, though one will always be designated as 'lead' doctor so that final decision on treatment can be assigned to a single person throughout their stay. There is usually more than one symptom recorded on each visit and patients are often prescribed more than one treatment on any visit (i.e. not just medication, but perhaps dietary suggestions, exercise, etc.).*
>
> *I want two data entry screens; the main one for visits and another one where I can add ongoing notes about individual patients.*
>
> *I nearly forgot, patients are identified by codes instead of by names because of the Data Protection Act. Each patient has been given a number between 1 and 100. The database must not hold identifiable patient data.*

BUILDING YOUR TABLES: CHECKLIST

For each table:

1. *Create data entry fields.*

2. *Assign data type and specify size and/or format.*

3. *Create captions where required.*

4. *Add any required properties, such as default value.*

5. *Assign primary key; ensure that foreign keys are present and set correctly.*

6. *Save and name the table.*

Field name (key)	Data type	Size/format	Caption
ConsultationKey (PK)	Auto Number	Default	Consultation code
DoctorKey (FK)	Number	Long Integer	Doctor
VisitKey (FK)	Number	Long Integer	Visit code
Lead	Yes/No	Default	Lead doctor?
ConsultationDate	Date/Time	Long Date	Consultation date
Comments	Long Text	Default	—

Table 15. The *Consultation* table.

Field name (key)	Data type	Size/format	Caption
DoctorKey (PK)	Auto Number	Default	Doctor code
DoctorName1	Short Text	50	First name
DoctorName2	Short Text	50	Last name
Comments	Long Text	Default	—

Table 16. The *Doctor* table.

Field name (key)	Data type	Size/format	Caption
IBDType (PK)	Short Text	40	IBD type
Comments	Long Text	Default	—

Table 17. The *IBDType* table.

Field name (key)	Data type	Size/format	Caption
Patient (PK)	Short Text	10	Patient code
IBDType (FK)	Short Text	40	IBD type
DateOfBirth	Date/Time	Long Date	Date of birth
Female	Yes/No	Default	Female?
PatientNotes	Long Text	Default	Patient notes

Table 18. The *Patient* table.

Field name (key)	Data type	Size/format	Caption
SymptomKey (PK)	Auto Number	Default	Symptom code
Symptom (FK)	Text	100	–
VisitKey (FK)	Number	Long Integer	Visit code
SymptomDate	Date/Time	Long Date	Symptom date
Comments	Long Text	Default	–

Table 19. The *Symptom* table.

Field name (key)	Data type	Size/format	Caption
Symptom (PK)	Short Text	100	–
Comments	Long Text	Default	–

Table 20. The *SymptomLookUp* table.

Field name (key)	Data type	Size/format	Caption
TreatmentKey (PK)	Auto Number	Default	Treatment code
Treatment (FK)	Short Text	100	–
VisitKey (FK)	Number	Long Integer	Visit code
TreatmentDate	Date/Time	Long Date	Tratment date
Comments	Long Text	Default	–

Table 21. The *Treatment* table.

Field name (key)	Data type	Size/format	Caption
Treatment (PK)	Short Text	100	–
Comments	Long Text	Default	–

Table 22. The *TreatmentLookUp* table.

Field name (key)	Data type	Size/format	Caption
VisitKey (PK)	Auto Number	Default	Visit code
Patient (FK)	Short Text	10	–
Routine	Yes/No	Default	–
VisitDate	Date/Time	Long Date	Visit date
DischargeDate	Date/Time	Long Date	Discharge date
Comments	Long Text	Default	–

Table 23. The *Visit* table.

ADDING THE RELATIONSHIPS: CHECKLIST

1. *For all relationships, create look–ups, which will automatically create drop–downs on any forms you subsequently build.*
2. *Where the drop–down needs to contain a person's name or alternative text to a code, set the drop–down to display the required data.*
3. *Finish all relationships in the Relationships window.*
4. *Save the relationships.*

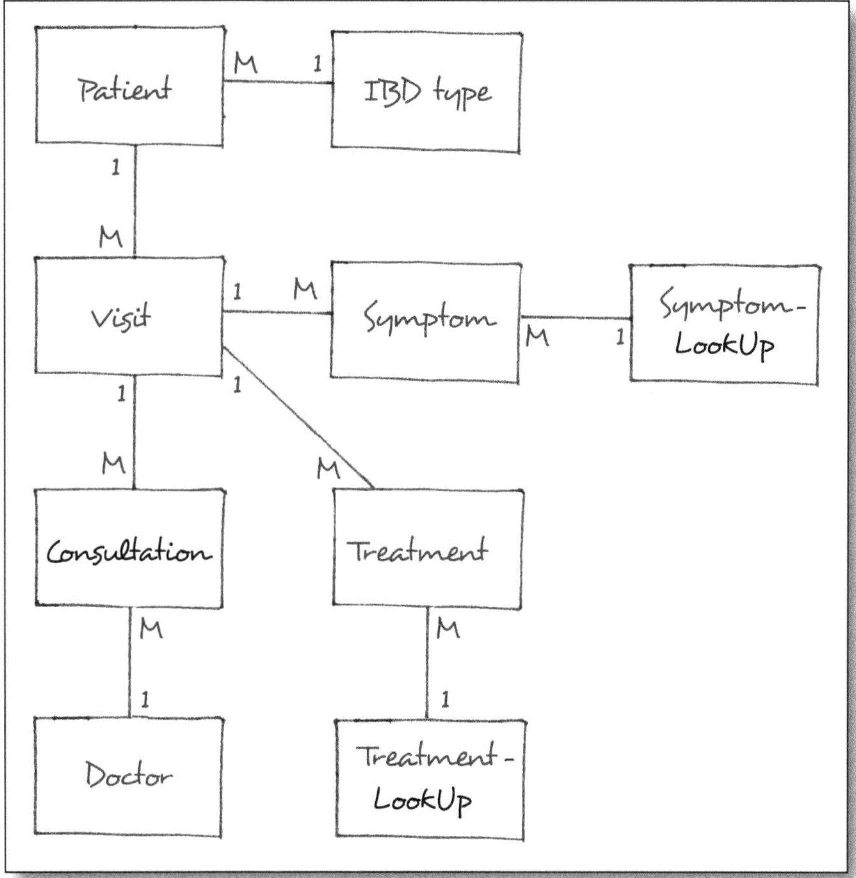

Figure 3. The research relational design showing the relationships that you will need to set.

Wherever you have a foreign key in a table, create a look–up to the table that holds the primary key (you should have worked out that this is what you have been doing by now). Don't forget to enable referential integrity and to finish all of the relationships off in the *Relationships* window.

In the *DoctorKey* drop–down in the *Consultation* table we want to see the doctors' names and not the code. You've already seen how to do this in the small business example, so you can go back and look up how to do this if you need to. *Patient* is a code only, remember, so we don't need to do this for the *Patient* drop–down in the *Visit* table.

Note that, apart from the *DoctorKey* look–up, where you need to see the name, you only need the primary key in the *Selected Fields* window when working through the *Lookup Wizard* for the other look–ups. Unless the primary key is an auto number field, sort it in ascending order when the wizard gets to that point.

Make sure that you have added and completed all of the relationships properly. Move the tables around to mirror the screenshot below so that you can see the relationships more clearly. If you have forgotten to add one (or more) then go back and add it/them.

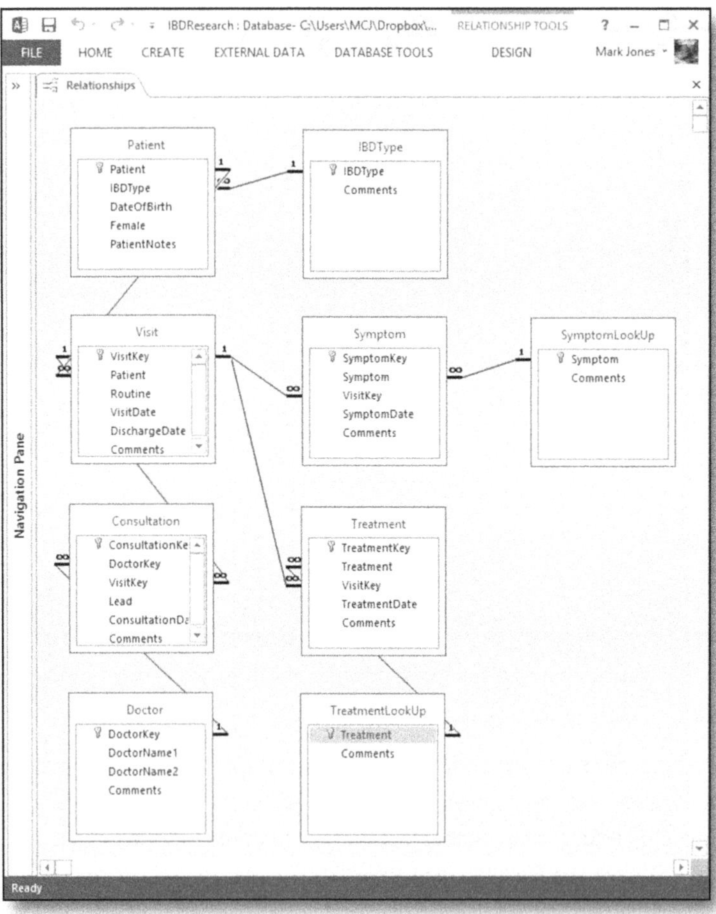

TEST YOUR DATABASE: CHECKLIST

1. Enter test data into each look–up table.

2. Enter one or two records into your main table, choosing data from all drop–downs.

3. Check the data in sub–tables.

4. If you have a sub–table where you expected a drop–down, or vice versa, then go back and see where you went wrong.

Just in case you don't know, the eight forms of IBD for the *IBDType* table are: Crohn's disease; ulcerative colitis; collagenous colitis; lymphocytic colitis; ischaemic colitis; diversion colitis; Behçet's disease; indeterminate colitis. For the other tables, you can just make it up.

SET UP YOUR DATA ENTRY FORMS: CHECKLIST

1. Create data entry form(s) using the Form Wizard option so as to create any required sub–forms automatically.

2. If you need more than one sub–form on a form, create and add these individually.

3. Fine–tune the data entry form to look and work how you want.

4. Save each form as you make changes to it.

The *Patient* form should cause no problems so, again, I'll leave you to it; but the *Visit* form will be a bit fiddly thanks to having multiple sub–forms. Let's just remind ourselves of the original, hand–drawn designs for the two forms. Bear in mind that both forms are missing fields, the need for which was surfaced after the designs had been drawn. This illustrates that designs are not set in stone and tend to change based on either remembering what you've forgotten or having a blinding flash of inspiration of how useful it could be to have the ability to record something you hadn't previously thought of. Databases are like that!

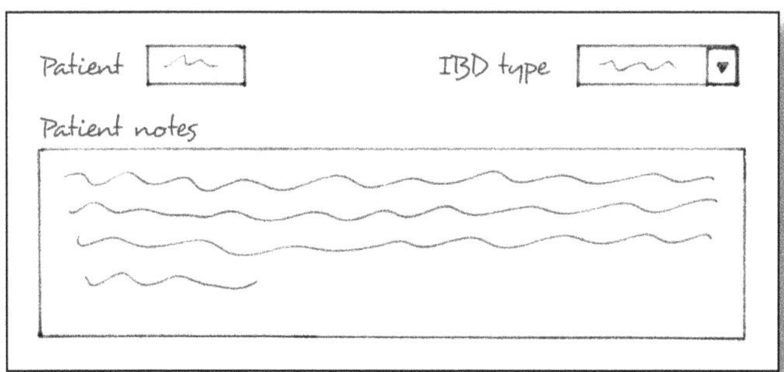

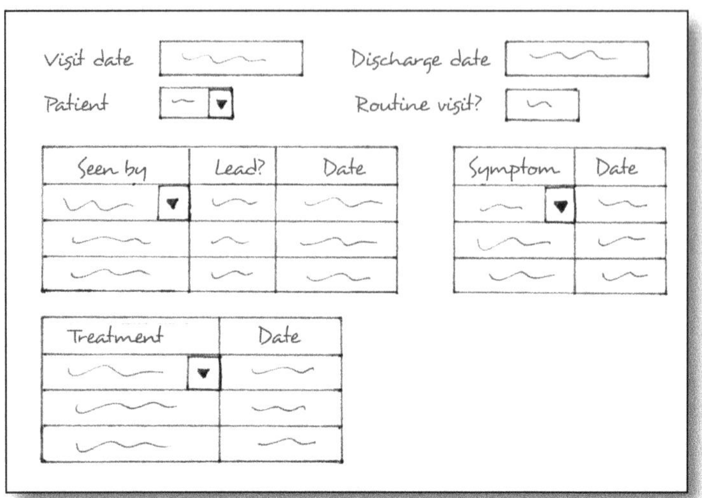

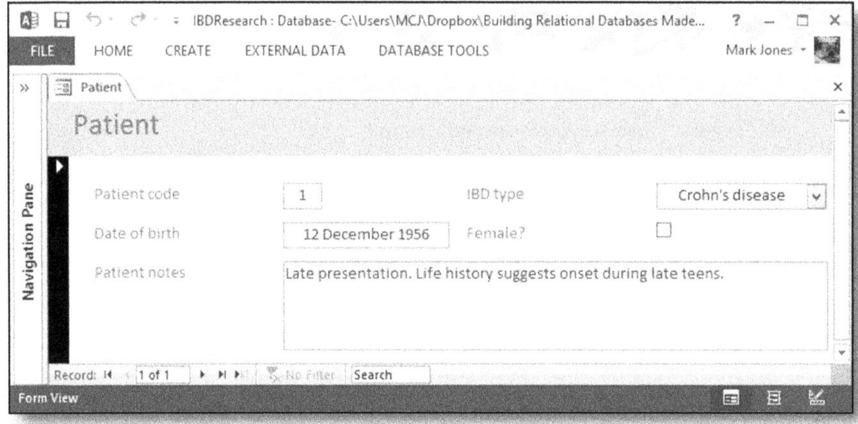

The Patient form could look something like the above. Now let's build the Visit form.

To build the Visit form:

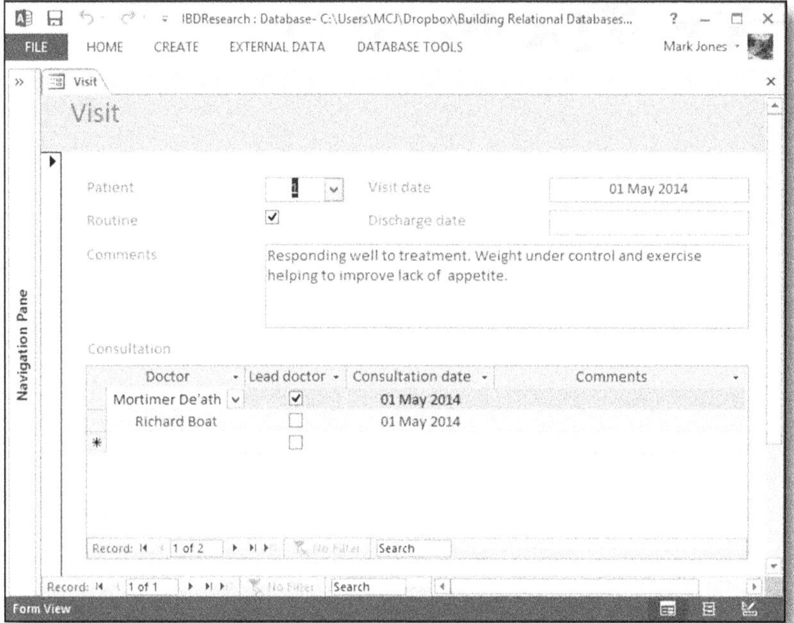

1. Use the *Form Wizard* to build a form and sub–form based on *Visit* (main form) and *Consultation* (sub–form) and name them as **Visit** and **ConsultationSubform**; this should look like the above screenshot when completed. The above are the only fields you need in your sub–form, remember. Rearrange things as you want and then close the form.

2. Do exactly the same as above, this time using the *Symptom* table for the sub–form. Don't bother doing any tidying up of the form in design view because we are not going to keep the main form for long. Name them as **Visit2** and **SymptomSubform**. Close the form

3. You may have guessed this already, but do exactly the same as above, this time using the *Treatment* table for the sub–form. Again, don't bother doing any tidying up of the form in design view. Name them as **Visit3** and **TreatmentSubform**. Close the form.

4. Right-click on *Visit2* in the *Navigation Pane* and select *Delete*, then do the same for *Visit3*.

5. Open the original *Visit* form in design view and drag *SymptomSubform* from the *Navigation Pane* across into the *Detail* section of the *Visit* form. Do the same for *TreatmentSubform*. Tidy up the sub–forms, including altering the tabbing, if required.

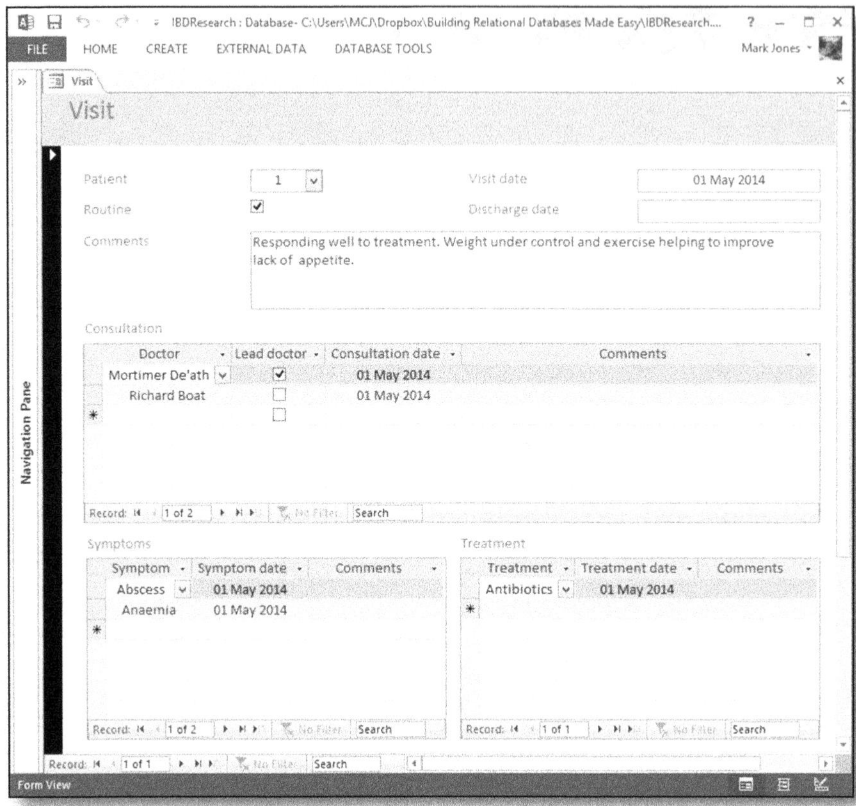

This, apart from requiring multiple forms and sub–forms, was a fairly straightforward database and there are no additional tasks required. To all intents and purposes, in that case, you have finished building the research database (except for navigation buttons and so on). You could add a button to open the Patient form based on the patient visit record you are looking at, but I'll leave that to you if you want to do it.

ENDNOTE

Although the building blocks for building any database are the same, it is with 'everything else' that the complexity creeps in. In the additional tasks, we've seen just a few of the things that can be done to make working with your database easier.

What you *could* do with your own Microsoft Access 2013 database is almost limitless. And that is why this book has stuck to just those additional tasks that tend to be common over many databases. That and introducing you to a few possibilities to get the old imagination juices going. Trying to cover everything that you could possibly do with your own database is an impossible task, which is why most 'how–to' books on Microsoft Access 2013 (and previous versions) tend to list the features, rather than tell you how to build a database.

It's also why many of those books are of little use unless you are already a hardened database developer. Without understanding the context of where you might want to use some of these features these (usually very large) books tend to either confuse or frighten off beginners – even some of those that say that they are for beginners.

I'm not saying that these books are of no use, however. In fact, what I'm going to suggest is that, if this book does not tell you how to do the specific additional tasks that you need done for your own database to be of use to you, then that's the time to move on to one of these all–singing, all–dancing 'everything you ever wanted to know about Microsoft Access 2013' books. After all, you're no longer a beginner – you've built a database or four by now.

This book has done the hard work of getting your database built to a usable state. The bells and whistles and the fine–tuning thereof will be different from database to database and I'm afraid I can't help you there. You've seen the database GP, but it's time to be refered to the Consultant now!

Just one last thing, this book (and the sister book, *Database Design Made Easy*), are available only as print–on–demand books so as to do just a little toward saving the planet and prevent cluttering up remainder bookshops. To do your bit, try to use recycled pixels when building and using your database. You know it makes sense.

Designing Databases Made Easy

M. Clinton Jones

ISBN: 978-1-909953-55-0
RRP: £26.99
Published by the Diogenes Academic Press
www.bristol-folk.co.uk

The presumption is that if you've read this current book, that you've already bought and used *Database Design Made Easy* so as to design your database prior to getting hands–on experience with Microsoft Access 2013.

If you haven't done this, even after all the heavy hints in this current book, then you really should because *Database Design Made Easy* uses a revolutionary new technique to design relational databases that anyone can follow, not just experts.

Most books on relational design force you to learn lots of esoteric theory before you can get on with the task of designing your database. *Database Design Made Easy*, however, gets you up and running from the very start. Instead of worrying about learning about relational design it tells you to get drawing. If you can draw your data entry screens, then the relational design magically takes care of itself.

Instead of tearing your hair out because you can't get to grips with normalisation, schema depictions, overlap preservation and denormalisation, whatever they are, *Database Design Made Easy* suggests sitting down with crayons and paper with a nice cup of tea and a bun. It's database design, Jim, but not as we've ever known it before.

Like *Building Relational Databases Made Easy*, this book is also printed on demand so as to save trees and help to keep remainders shops free from too much clutter. Printing on demand means that the book is only manufactured at the point at which you buy it. Yes, you know it makes sense.

Space for your own development notes

Space for your own development notes

Space for your own development notes

Space for your own development notes

Space for your own development notes

Space for your own development notes

www.ingramcontent.com/pod-product-compliance
Ingram Content Group UK Ltd.
Pitfield, Milton Keynes, MK11 3LW, UK
UKHW012055240726
13965UKWH00004B/1300

9 781909 953567